Samuel

Encountering the king-maker

ROGER ELLSWORTH

SERIES EDITOR: SIMON J ROBINSON

DayOne

© Day One Publications 2006

First printed 2006

ISBN 978-1-84625-039-2

9 781846 250392 >

British Library Cataloguing in Publication Data available

Published by Day One Publications
Ryelands Road, Leominster, HR6 8NZ
Telephone 01568 613 740   FAX 01568 611 473

email—sales@dayone.co.uk
web site—www.dayone.co.uk

Designed by Steve Devane and printed by Gutenberg Press, Malta.

CONTENTS

APPRECIATIONS

'Roger Ellsworth's book is an extremely relevant and helpful study in the life of Samuel, a much-neglected Old Testament character. It is an extremely practical, pastoral and, most important of all, Christ-exalting-character study at its best and an invaluable addition to a promising series.'

Derek Prime

'Roger Ellsworth has written an intensely useable, well arranged approach to the truths presented in 1 Samuel. Insightful biblical interpretation and powerful theological truths are compellingly portrayed and carefully explained throughout the book. Moreover, the book is filled with rich spiritual applications. I heartily commend Face2Face with Samuel for a wide audience of readers.'

Dr David S. Dockery,

President, Union University, Jackson, Tennessee

Dedicated to my dear friends, John and Carol Brandt

Introduction

Welcome to the world of dirt roads and oxcarts, cattle and sheep, sandals and robes! Welcome to the world of Samuel!

Who was Samuel? One of the most important men in the history of the nation of Israel! For a long time Israel was ruled by 'judges' (see the book by that name!), but after Samuel she was governed by kings. Samuel occupies, then, a unique position in the history of his nation. We might call him a bridge from one era to another.

But we are not taking this 'face2face' look at Samuel because we are interested in historical uniqueness. It is rather because this man can help us with life in general and with the main thing in life.

And what is the main thing in life? We must be clear-headed about this. It is knowing the God who made us through the means he has established for knowing him. That 'means' is God's plan of salvation.

This plan was introduced into human history by God himself after Adam and Eve sinned against him. It consists of his Son, Jesus Christ, taking our humanity. In that humanity he did what Adam and Eve failed to do, that is, live in obedience to God. And in that humanity, he went to the cross where he received the penalty Adam and Eve deserved. There he received the full measure of the wrath of God.

Why should we be interested in this? Because Adam's sin is our sin! And its penalty—eternal separation from God—is our penalty! It comes down to this: that penalty is either ours or Christ's on our behalf. If we repent of our sins and trust completely in what Jesus did on the cross, we will never have to bear the wrath of God ourselves. If we refuse to trust Christ, that wrath will be ours to bear.

Nothing could possibly be more important than the salvation that God provided in Jesus. We must be vitally interested in this, or be for ever lost. The Lord Jesus himself pointedly asked: 'For what profit is it to a man if he gains the whole world, and loses his own soul? Or what will a man give in exchange for his soul?' (Matthew 16:26).

Those who are interested in salvation cannot help but be interested in the Bible, which is 'Salvation's History Book.' We might as well try to tell grandparents not to be interested in their grandchildren as tell the saved not to be interested in the Bible. And to be interested in the Bible is to be interested in Samuel, who played a significant role in the drama of salvation.

• As a prophet, Samuel declared the truth of God to his people, the centrepiece of which was God's saving grace. The eighteenth-century American theologian Jonathan Edwards said: 'The main business of this succession of prophets was to foreshow Christ, and the glorious redemption he was to accomplish, and so to prepare the way for his coming.'[1]

• As a priest, Samuel offered sacrifices to God on behalf of his people, and those sacrifices themselves foreshadowed Jesus who would be the perfect sacrifice for sinners.

• As a judge, Samuel reflected the kingly rule of the Lord Jesus Christ in the hearts of his people. That kingly rule was, of course, even more perfectly displayed in the great King David, whom Samuel was commanded to anoint.

• As a devoted follower of God, Samuel demonstrated the life of faithfulness and service that all believers in Christ are to practise.

So I do not apologize for asking you to join me for a 'face2face' look at Samuel. Imagine it! A man without a cell phone or a computer having something to say to us! Can it be? Come and see!

Notes

1 **Jonathan Edwards,** *The Works of Jonathan Edwards* (Edinburgh: The Banner of Truth Trust, 1976), vol. i, p. 552.

1 The mystery of God's ways

1 Samuel 1:1–18

Lots of us love a good mystery. The more mysterious, the better! We delight in the twists and turns of the plot as a detective doggedly follows one clue after the other and finally nabs the culprit. But many prefer that God not be mysterious. We like for him to 'keep us up to speed' by explaining himself every step of the way. Although the Bible tells us that this life will always be like peering through a dark glass (1 Corinthians 13:12), we often find ourselves desiring the transparency that is reserved for eternity.

MYSTERY AND MISERY

Samuel's story begins in mystery, and God was the one who was being mysterious.

Elkanah and Hannah, Samuel's parents, were for a long time vexed and perplexed by Hannah's inability to conceive. They desperately desired for her to have children, but the Lord had closed her womb (v. 5).

There is quite enough mystery in that fact alone. Why would God withhold from Hannah the one thing that Jewish women of that time more earnestly craved than anything else?

But the mystery deepens and darkens. Elkanah's other wife,

Peninnah—she who never had any difficulty conceiving—never missed a chance to ridicule Hannah and make her feel like a failure.

It's not hard to figure who was the better of these two women. Peninnah was obviously cruel and unfeeling, but, as the first two chapters of 1 Samuel make clear, Hannah was a godly, sensitive and loving woman.

Here we have, then, a wicked woman who had been blessed with children and a godly woman who had not. We are peering into a dark mystery. Why should a godly person suffer such disappointment and heartbreak? The other prong to this mystery is why should wicked people be more blessed than the godly? It's not that the latter do not want people without God to be blessed; it's rather a matter of why those without God often seem to be more blessed than the righteous. Shouldn't serving God count for something?

The author leaves no doubt about it. Peninnah deliberately tried to make life difficult for Hannah and admirably succeeded. Hannah was miserable. It was long misery ('year after year'—v. 7), and it was deep misery ('wept', 'did not eat', 'bitterness of soul', 'wept in anguish', 'sorrowful spirit'—vv. 7,10,15).

PRAYER AND PEACE

We must admire Hannah. She could have been content merely to settle down in the misery and cry: 'Woe is me.' It is possible to enjoy our misery! But Hannah, wise woman that she was, refused to do so. She fled to the refuge of prayer and found comfort there.

Dale Ralph Davis suggests that Hannah dared to believe 'that the broken heart of a relatively obscure woman in the hill country of Ephraim' mattered to God.[1] So she began to pray. How she prayed! She didn't mechanically mouth a few set clichés, but poured her heart out to the Lord (v. 15). She told him of the depth of her anguish. She told him the great desire of her heart for a son.

Good always comes from such praying, and so it was with Hannah. The most obvious good she received is stated in the words: 'It came to pass in the process of time that Hannah conceived and bore a son' (v. 20).

But the fact is that Hannah received good before she ever conceived. Verse 18 tells us that after she prayed 'her face was no longer sad'. Even before the trial was removed she received peace regarding it.

A woman bearing a son after it seemed impossible for her to do so! It calls to mind another Jewish woman centuries later. She too was faced with the impossible—bearing a son without a human father. But the same God who had no difficulty in giving the barren Hannah a son also had no trouble in giving the virgin Mary a son. As the angel said to Mary: 'For with God nothing will be impossible' (Luke 1:37).

We can easily relate to Hannah staring at life's mysteries and feeling misery. We all have circumstances that make us hammer heaven with that anguished word—'Why?' Sickness comes, finances fail, friendships fracture, loved ones die, and the faith which is supposed to sustain us is often ridiculed and scorned. We ask 'why' a lot, but we seldom get our 'why's answered to our satisfaction. Hannah's experience certainly doesn't give us all the answers, but it does give us something of real value. It tells us how to live with our 'why's until they finally disintegrate in the glory of God's presence.

REFUSE TO LEAVE GOD OUT

When a disappointment or a difficulty arises, many explain it by saying God had nothing to do with it.

All parents know the helpless feeling of not being able to keep our children from harm and danger. We try, but there's always that unforeseen something that pops up to injure our children. Many people see God in the same way. As far as they are concerned, he is the great concerned parent in the sky. While he tries very hard to keep his children out of harm's way, something invariably pops up to take him by surprise.

Such people expect finally to confront God and ask why they had to face some great trial. And they fully expect him to shrug his shoulders, shake his head in dismay and say: 'We tried to prevent it, but we just couldn't. Hope you understand.'

The image of a well-meaning deity who bumbles and fumbles his way along has become indelibly etched in the minds of many through the books and movies of the last several years. We envision a God who struggles along with incompetent staff, computer foul-ups and unforeseen circumstances. But a well-meaning, helpless God is not the explanation for Hannah's disappointment. Scripture flatly says she was not able to bear children because 'the LORD had closed her womb' (vv. 5–6). We can wonder all we want about why God would do such a thing, but the Bible closes the option of saying God had nothing to do with it.

The Bible tells us God is sovereign, that not a sparrow falls that he doesn't know about, that not a single hair of our heads goes unnoticed or uncounted. However we choose to explain our suffering in this life, one thing we can't say is that it takes place without God's knowledge or permission. This truth greatly bothers some, but it should rather comfort us to know that nothing can come to us that our loving heavenly Father doesn't allow.

REFUSE TO BE BITTER TOWARDS GOD

Some fall into another trap. They know God is not a helpless parent who wrings his hands in despair over the trials of his children, but they find themselves feeling bitter towards God. They may even console themselves by thinking they can get even with him: 'Since God allowed this to happen to me, I'll punish him by not going to church.'

All who feel such bitterness lose sight of one great fact—God sends trials and disappointments because he has far nobler purposes in mind than we can possibly comprehend, purposes that always have the best interests of his children at heart.

Hannah could have been bitter about her disappointment, but she wasn't. She had 'bitterness of soul' (v. 10), but that only means her childlessness was painful for her. It doesn't mean she was angry at God. If she had been bitter towards God she would never have referred to herself three times as the Lord's 'maidservant' (v. 11), that is, a woman who exists solely for the purpose of carrying out the desires of her master. Hannah obviously regarded the Lord as her Master.

What mattered most to Hannah, therefore, was not what she wanted, but rather what God wanted. And that was far greater than Hannah ever imagined! God desired a Samuel to lead a sinful nation back to himself. It was by closing Hannah's womb for several years that God got his Samuel. If Samuel had come quickly and easily to Hannah, she would not have been inclined to feel an extra measure of gratitude, and without that gratitude she would not have dedicated her son to the Lord.

As a result of enduring the trial without bitterness, Hannah discovered that God indeed had a far greater purpose in mind, namely, the good of the whole nation. She also discovered that he had her own interests at heart. Hannah was rewarded for enduring the trial God sent to her. She was undoubtedly brought to a higher level of commitment and trust than she ever occupied before. And she ended up having three more sons and two daughters (2:21).

It's often hard for us to accept, but our God does all things well. He does indeed 'work all things together for good' for his children (Romans 8:28). He will never have to apologize to any of his children for the trials he has sent their way. But many of us will have to apologize to him for questioning his love and wisdom.

REFUSE TO GIVE UP ON GOD

The third thing for us to see in Hannah is a woman who refused to give up on God for not easing her disappointment.

Hannah didn't know why God had allowed her to experience the disappointment of barrenness, but there were some things she did know. She knew this trial was not necessarily permanent, that God had the power to lift the trial. And she knew that prayer is the channel God uses to employ his power on behalf of his people.

What trial do you carry today? What disappointment troubles and vexes you? Does it seem like God has forgotten you in the midst of your troubles? Take comfort from knowing the trial can be eased through believing prayer.

The praying of Hannah was an essential part of God giving Samuel to his people. We can rest assured that prayer will play a significant role in God doing great things for his people today.

When God gave Hannah the son for whom she had so fervently prayed, she gave him the name 'Samuel', which means 'heard by God'. If we want to be heard, we must ask. May God help us not to fall under the terrible indictment of James: 'You do not have because you do not ask' (James 4:2).

God may not deal with us as he did with Hannah, but we certainly must deal with him as Hannah did. He may not see fit to remove the trial from us, any more than he saw fit to remove a trial that greatly troubled the apostle Paul. But if God decides to leave the trial, we can rest assured he will remove its crushing sadness by giving us the grace to bear it (2 Corinthians 12:7–10).

When trials come, we must go! We must go to God in prayer, tell him how deeply it hurts and ask him either to remove it or to give us grace to bear it. And we must ask him to help us trust that he has a wise purpose in his mind and our best interests in his heart.

The devil will always be quick to assure us that it is not so: 'God does not have our best interests at heart! The trial proves it!' But the cross of Christ is ever the answer. The fact that God nailed his Son there to receive the wrath of God in the stead of sinners for ever answers how God feels about his people.

For further study ▶

FOR FURTHER STUDY

1. Read Psalm 73 for another example of a believer who seemed less blessed than unbelievers. How did Asaph find comfort?
2. Job is the classic example of a saint of God experiencing great difficulty. How did he find relief? Read Job 42:1–6.

TO THINK ABOUT AND DISCUSS

1. In what respect do you find God's ways to be mysterious? Why do you think sometimes works in such mysterious ways (see Isaiah 55:8–9)? Think about the times in your own life when you have been perplexed by God's ways. What does he teach us through such times?
2. Look at the way in which Hannah handled her disappointment. How does it compare to your own attitude when things do not go as you would like them to? Think about ways in which you can make your mindset more like Hannah's.

Notes

1 **Dale Ralph Davis,** *Looking on the Heart: 1 Samuel 1–14* (Grand Rapids: Baker Books, 1994), p. 19.

2 Godly parents in ungodly times

1 Samuel 1:19–2:11

Let's try to walk a mile or two in Hannah's sandals. See her now as she makes her way down the dusty road from Ramah to Shiloh. With her are her husband Elkanah, and her young son Samuel. The tabernacle of the Lord is at Shiloh. Eli, the high priest, and his sons are there. The ark of the covenant is there as well.

Hannah and Elkanah have been to Shiloh many times for the various religious festivals conducted there, but this trip is different. Hannah has made a special vow to the Lord that Samuel will be devoted to the Lord's service all of his life, and the time has now come for her and Elkanah to leave him with Eli at the tabernacle.

THE GRATITUDE OF A GODLY MOTHER

Great gratitude must have welled up within as Hannah thought about what the Lord had done for her. When it looked as if she was destined to be childless, he had heard her prayer and had given her and Elkanah their precious son. She did not have to make a special commitment of Samuel to the Lord, but her heart of gratitude would allow her to do no other. The heart touched by the mercy of God always desires to do more than what is required. So it was with Hannah. Her special commitment was the tangible way she found to express her thanksgiving to the God who had so stunningly blessed her.

THE CONCERN OF A GODLY MOTHER

But the tide of gratitude no sooner reached its peak than another tide rolled up to slam against it, a tide of pain at the thought of separation from her beloved son and uncertainty about what lay ahead of him.

The searing reality of separation would have been difficult enough. Few things in life are more difficult than being separated from those who are near and dear to us. All of us who have laid loved ones to rest know the sharp thrust of that dagger. But the pain of separation was coupled with this business of uncertainty about the future.

These were not good days in Israel. Moral laxity abounded on every side. It seemed that responsibility and discipline had fallen to the ground to be swept away with the rubbish. The laws of God were treated as mere relics that no longer had meaning or usefulness. The general tone and tenor of that day was for individuals to make up their own laws as they went along.

Why would the tattered moral fibre of Israel be of concern to Hannah as she trudged along the path to Shiloh? It would seem that the best thing she could do to protect her son from the onslaught of moral permissiveness was what she and her husband were doing. What better place for Samuel to be protected from evil and nurtured in the things of God than the tabernacle of God?

But, alas, the moral decline had reached even into the very tabernacle of God and tainted the priests! Hophni and Phinehas, the sons of Eli, were disgusting moral specimens (2:12–17). Furthermore, these things were known throughout the nation of Israel. The scandalous behaviour of Hophni and Phinehas, along with the weakness and timidity of Eli, were written large before the eyes of the people of Israel.

Hannah must have wondered if she and her husband were doing the right thing in leaving Samuel at the very tabernacle where wickedness and weakness abounded. They seemed to be taking their young son into the very teeth of the storm. How could their son turn out to be godly in the midst of such circumstances?

THE PRAYER OF A GODLY MOTHER

At the nub of it, Hannah's current situation was of the same cloth as that which she had previously experienced. When she was childless, her situation looked utterly bleak and hopeless, but God had intervened and given her a child. She begins her prayer by celebrating this: 'I rejoice in your salvation' (2:1). In this context, the word 'salvation' refers to God delivering her from barrenness.

A little later, Hannah celebrates the great power of God by saying: 'There is none besides you, nor is there any rock like our God' (2:2). We associate rocks with strength, and God is, according to Hannah, a rock like no other. In other words, he is unrivalled in strength.

Hannah knew that this powerful God who had been at work in her life would be at work in the life of her son. She was taking young Samuel into a situation that was so difficult that it looked as if it would be impossible for him to turn out right, but God's strength was sufficient even for that situation.

Hannah also took refuge in the knowledge that God had securely established this earth (2:8), and that nothing can destroy it until he himself brings it to its appointed end. Furthermore, she found peace in the knowledge that God can guard the steps of his people even while they walk in this wicked world (2:9).

Hannah also understood about the future victory of God over all evil. 'There is none holy like the LORD,' says Hannah (2:2). Then she adds: 'For the LORD is the God of knowledge; and by him actions are weighed' (v. 3). The latter statement tells us that God knows all about evil. None of it has escaped his notice. He has seen it all. The former statement tells us he is not ambivalent or neutral about it. God's holiness means he is not only untainted by evil himself, but that he has sworn eternal hostility against it. God's holiness guarantees that he will finally judge all evil-doers and will eliminate all evil.

This truth would be powerfully manifested in Israel in Samuel's early years. Evil flourished for such a long time that the people no doubt thought they were getting away with it, but God suddenly moved sharply to curtail it and to bring the people back to a state of spiritual vitality.

And the judgements God uses to curtail evil in this world simply foreshadow the final judgement in which 'The adversaries of the LORD shall be broken in pieces' (2:10), and 'the wicked shall be silent in darkness' (2:9).

We who are Christian parents know what it is to feel the

swelling tide of uncertainty over the future of our children roll over us. We also live in trying times—times of moral laxity and confusion, times when God's laws are scorned and disdained, times in which people make up their own rules as they go along. Yes, our times have even seen wickedness and moral weakness reach all the way into the Christian ministry.

All of this makes the rearing of godly children extremely difficult and challenging. Sometimes it seems impossible. All the different aspects of our society seem to have come together in a gigantic conspiracy to undermine the morality of our children, and Christian parents don't always know how to respond. We know we can't keep our children from the moral contamination of our day by locking them up and throwing away the key. But what can we do?

Hannah can help us. She knew all about the flood-tide of wickedness in Israel and at the tabernacle. She knew all about the pathetic weakness of Eli. But she also knew some things that can help all parents in fearful times.

THE PRESENT SUFFICIENCY OF GOD

As we look at her prayer, we find only a hint or two about the evil circumstances of that time, but a lot about God. 'The LORD' appears eight times and 'the LORD'S' once. Pronouns for God occur fourteen times. That makes a total of twenty-three times that Hannah makes mention of God in a prayer that takes up only ten verses.

Hannah may have glanced at her circumstances, but she gazed at her God! We can easily reverse this pattern—gazing at our problems and circumstances and glancing at God. The object at which we gaze will occupy our minds, and that which occupies our minds will govern and control our lives. If we gaze at our problems, we will constantly feel overwhelmed, but if we gaze at God we will find the resources we need for facing the challenges of life.

What did Hannah see as she gazed at God? She saw his power to deliver and preserve his people. Sometimes it seems that the power of evil is so great that everything that is nailed down is going to come loose and that the very earth itself will be destroyed. When the whole world seems to be tottering from the power of evil, rest in this—the strength of sin is great, but the strength of God is greater.

THE FUTURE VICTORY OF GOD

God is the preserver of his people in evil times. He will guard their steps until their work here is done, and he will then take them home to heaven where they shall be so perfectly preserved that nothing will be able to touch them again. The other truth shown in Hannah's prayer is that God is the great leveller. Evil may flourish so much that it appears to have triumphed, but God is going to level it to the ground. He has sworn to bring evil-doers low and to lift his people high.

The best thing Christian parents can do for their children in these evil days is to hold before them these truths. We should labour to make sure they understand the greatness of God. We should labour to help them see that God preserves his people. We should labour to help them grasp the truth that God sees evil and will judge it. Essentially it comes to this—if we who are parents are to do well in rearing our children, we must remember great men and great women have great parents, and great parents have a great God.

FOR FURTHER STUDY

1. In Luke 1:46–55 we read Mary's great song of praise. How does it resemble Hannah's?

2. Read 1 Thessalonians 4:13–18 and think about what it teaches us about God's future victory.

TO THINK ABOUT AND DISCUSS

1. What brings you special gratitude as you recall the Lord's dealings with you? What things has God done in your life for which you can and should be especially grateful? Think about your relationship with him; your personal circumstances; your church life; your work life.

2. What brings today's Christian parents special concern? What particular things? How should they face these things? How can those who are not Christians help and support those who are in these days?

3 The approaching dawn

1 Samuel 2:12–36

Count them! Samuel's name is mentioned only three times in the above verses (vv. 18,21,26). The remaining verses, excluding the cheering note about additional children for Hannah (vv. 18–21), consist of a dreary account of the moral and spiritual darkness that had enveloped the priesthood of Israel. Primarily, it is the account of those two nasty specimens, Hophni and Phinehas, and the helplessness of their father Eli.

Dale Ralph Davis writes: 'It is a bleak hour indeed when the light of the world is part of the darkness.'[1] While there have been many times in which the supposed light was part of the darkness, there has never been a time in which this was more the case. Yes, there have been times to match it, but none to surpass it.

The priests of Israel were supposed to be the light of the world. They were supposed to disseminate the knowledge of God to a dark world, but, tragically, the light was part of the darkness.

ELI AND HIS SONS
What were Hophni and Phinehas doing? The text leaves little

to the imagination. These moral wrecks were confiscating from worshippers what was to be offered to the Lord (vv. 12–17). And, astoundingly enough, they were engaging in sexual immorality 'with the women who assembled at the door of the tabernacle of meeting' (v. 22).

Give old Eli some credit. He was able to muster enough courage to confront his sons with their outrageous conduct. They were sinning against God, and Eli tried to show them the seriousness of what they were doing: 'If a man sins against the LORD, who will intercede for him?' (v. 25).

But we cannot give him much credit, because he refused to do that which the situation demanded, namely, remove his sons from the priesthood. His words carried no weight with his sons. They did not know the Lord (v. 12). Spiritual truth means nothing to those who are spiritually dead. And there was another element at work in their complete disregard for the truth—God wanted to kill them (v. 25)! They continued to live only because God was allowing them to ripen for judgement.

We are confronted here with the reality of judicial hardening. God judges those who harden their hearts against him by hardening their hearts even more, thus making his judgement even more just.

A PROPHET AND ELI

In the midst of all this high-handed sinning and hardening, God sent a hard-hitting prophet to Eli. This man had some bite! He delivered a powerful four-point sermon: God had been good to the house of Eli (vv. 27–28); Eli had been shockingly ungrateful (v. 29); God promised severe judgement (vv. 30–34); and God promised to raise up a faithful priest (vv. 35–36).

GOD AND SAMUEL

We began by noting that Samuel is mentioned only three times in these verses. It is interesting to observe the placement of these references. It looks like this:

The wickedness of Hophni and Phinehas is emphasised (vv. 12–17).

Samuel is mentioned twice (vv. 18,21).

The wickedness of Hophni and Phinehas is emphasised (vv. 22–25).

Samuel is mentioned (v. 26).

What are we to make of this? Dale Ralph Davis offers this conclusion: 'It must have seemed to many like there was no hope of improvement, no exit from the night. But in the middle of it all the text keeps whispering, "Don't forget Samuel ..."'[2]

In the midst of that darkness, it must have seemed to people of faith that God was not doing anything. But he was doing something—he was raising up a child! That doesn't sound like much, but it proved to be a lot. Samuel would make a huge difference. God's seemingly insignificant work was anything but!

Centuries later would find the people of Israel once again enveloped in deep darkness. God had not spoken for a period of 400 years. Faith was sputtering as religious formalism abounded. And once again God's answer was to send a child: 'And she brought forth her firstborn Son, and wrapped him in swaddling cloths, and laid him in a manger' (Luke 2:7).

How significant could it be that a child had been born in a manger in Bethlehem? When he died some thirty years later, it was to receive the wrath of God in the stead of sinners so those sinners would never have to experience that wrath themselves. That child was Jesus. That child made a difference!

KEEP IN MIND THE ALL-SEEING GOD

This passage reminds us that nothing, absolutely nothing, is hidden from God's eyes! He was aware of the atrocities of Hophni and Phinehas and the ineptitude of their father. There is no crevice in which sin can lurk that hides it from the penetrating gaze of God.

KEEP IN MIND THE DANGER OF PROFESSION WITHOUT POSSESSION

The sad account of the house of Eli is very distressing. The distress comes from the solemn reminder that a religious vocation and religious trappings do not secure a right relationship with God. One can be very near religious things and very far from God. The Lord Jesus himself offered this stern assessment of the religious leaders of his day:

> This people honors me with their lips,
>
> But their heart is far from me
>
> (Mark 7:6b).

Every religious leader would do well to remember that, apart from the regenerating grace of God working in his heart, the very same words apply to him.

KEEP IN MIND THE FAITHFULNESS OF CHRIST

Every glimpse of corrupt religious leadership in the Bible should drive us gratefully to consider the Lord Jesus Christ, who faithfully discharged the redemptive work assigned to him by the Father. No one has ever encountered larger difficulties than did the Lord Jesus in fulfilling his mission. But he overcame them all and offered to God a life that was unsullied and unstained by sin.

KEEP LOOKING UP

The days described in the first two chapters of 1 Samuel were dark indeed, but Samuel was coming! Our own times offer us more than enough darkness, but Jesus is coming! And when he comes, the darkness will give way to glorious light.

FOR FURTHER STUDY

1. Look at 1 Samuel 8:1–3, 2 Samuel 14:1–15:37 and 1 Kings 1:1–53 for additional instances of fathers who had rebellious children. Who were these fathers?
2. Malachi 1:6–2:9 gives us another instance of priests failing. What were they doing?

TO THINK ABOUT AND DISCUSS

1. How should God's people respond if they are blessed with a faithful gospel ministry?
2. What is your response to the fact that nothing is hidden from God? What impact should knowledge of this fact make to our lives: our actions, and our thoughts?

Notes

1 **Davis,** p. 29.
2 **Davis,** p. 31.

4 Samuel the prophet

1 Samuel 3:1–4:1

It is a charming and entertaining story. The tabernacle has been shut down for the day, and Eli and the child Samuel have gone to bed. But God is not through conducting business for the day. He speaks to Samuel in the night, and, after some initial confusion, Samuel responds and begins his prophetic ministry.

But this account is not here to entertain us. It presents a matter of momentous importance. In his dealings with the child Samuel, God was providing his people with something they had sorely lacked and urgently needed—the ministry of a prophet.

THE PROPHET NEEDED

God has no greater gift than to give than his word, and no greater judgement to send than withholding his word.

This passage begins by telling us that God was withholding his word from Israel: 'And the word of the LORD was rare in those days; there was no widespread revelation' (v. 1). It was not a matter of there being absolutely no prophecy at all. It was rather that prophecy was very infrequent and sporadic. Chapter 2 mentions a man of God who delivered a prophecy to

Eli (2:27–36), but that was just one prophecy to one man. A far cry from prophecy flourishing! Ongoing prophecy that spoke to the whole nation was at this point a thing of the past.

How had Israel reached this sad and low state? The answer is ready at hand. The people had stopped listening to God. They had the laws he gave to Moses, and they knew all about the many instances in which God had spoken, but they did not prize these things. They had disregarded his laws. They had forgotten the glorious things he had said. Israel was the one nation with a speaking God, but her people were living as if he had not spoken at all.

The very tabernacle in which Eli and Samuel lay down to sleep was a testimony to the fact that God had spoken to Israel, as were 'the lamp of God' and 'the ark of God' (v. 3). The author's mention of the lamp going out may have been his way of indicating both the lateness of the hour and the immense tragedy of a silent God. When God does not speak, spiritual light flickers and fails!

THE PROPHET CALLED

Suddenly Samuel hears his name called. Old, nearly blind, heavy-set Eli would often have needed help in the night. Therefore it is not surprising that Samuel assumed it was Eli who called. But, no, it was not Eli (vv. 4–5). The same thing happened a second time (v. 6) and a third (v. 8).

Eli finally realized what was happening. God was speaking to the boy! So Eli sent Samuel back to his bed with instructions. If God spoke again, Samuel was to say: 'Speak, LORD, for your servant hears' (v. 9).

God did speak again, calling Samuel's name twice, and

Samuel responded as he had been instructed (v. 10). At this point Samuel was given his first message to declare, one that echoed that which was declared by the aforementioned prophet (2:27–36).

THE PROPHET USED

Having received this message, Samuel 'lay down until morning' (3:15). How much he slept we do not know. When day dawned, he would have a solemn task to perform!

He received his opportunity when Eli asked him to tell what the Lord had revealed (3:16–17).

Samuel's response set the tone for his whole ministry and the standard for all succeeding prophets and preachers: 'Then Samuel told him everything, and hid nothing from him' (3:18). The apostle Paul so admirably lived up to this standard that he was able to say to the Ephesian elders: 'I have not shunned to declare to you the whole counsel of God' (Acts 20:27).

From that small and faithful beginning, Samuel's prophesying would grow until the entire nation realized 'that Samuel had been established as a prophet of the LORD' (3:20) and it touched and nourished the whole nation (4:1). Samuel's ministry was effective only because the Lord 'let none of his words fall to the ground' (3:19).

REVERING THE GOD OF SAMUEL

We have often heard the maxim: The main thing is to keep the main thing the main thing.

We can easily lose sight of this when we deal with the great stories of the Bible. The story of the call of Samuel can find us focusing more on little Samuel than on God, thus forgetting that God is the hero of every story of the Bible. We deprive ourselves of significant blessing and comfort when we shuttle God to one side. Nothing so helps the people of God as the renewed vision of their Lord.

One of the primary insights this passage gives regarding God is into the kindness of his heart. In calling Samuel, he was being kind to the nation of Israel. He could have left her without his word, and no one could accuse him of injustice. But he renewed his word through Samuel.

The Lord was also being kind to Samuel. It is always a kindness when the Lord puts us in his service. And was it not extremely kind and gracious of God to persist with Samuel, not speaking just once and then withdrawing, but speaking again and again?

REJOICING IN THE INDESTRUCTIBILITY OF GOD'S WORD

What does this event have to do with us? Why should we concern ourselves with it at all? Preachers often make the point that God calls today as he called Samuel so long ago, and we must be ready to answer his call. It is true—God is a calling God. He calls sinners and grants them spiritual life and faith in his Son. He ever calls his people to greater faith and service. He also calls some to preach the gospel.

But there is a uniqueness about the call of Samuel that we must not miss. The Lord was calling a prophet for himself, one who would declare his word. The fact that he did so at a time when wickedness was so prevalent shows us that God will not allow his word to be overcome by evil. God sustains his own cause. The truth that we should carry away from this passage, therefore, is the indestructibility of God's word.

Centuries later would find many Jews in captivity in Babylon. That would also be a time in which evil would appear invincibly strong, but those people would find comfort in these words from God:

> The grass withers, the flower fades,
>
> But the word of our God stands for ever
>
> (Isaiah 40:8).

The point at which Samuel's experience speaks so pointedly to us, then, is this: God will sustain and preserve his word.

HEARING THE WORD OF GOD

The fact that God sustains his word does not relieve us of responsibility. The call of Samuel reminds us that we must be ever eager to receive God's word. John Trapp observes: 'A hearing ear is a sweet mercy: a heavy ear, a grievous judgment.'[1]

We must, therefore, be constantly on guard against the terrible malady about which the author of Hebrews warned his readers, namely, dullness in hearing God's word (Hebrews 5:11). Instead we must choose to obey the words of the apostle James by being 'swift to hear' (James 1:19).

FAITHFULLY PROCLAIMING THE WORD OF GOD

We cannot leave the call of Samuel without drawing yet another conclusion: Preachers who hold back part of the truth of God in order to ingratiate themselves with their hearers are unworthy of their name and stain their calling.

On the other hand, those who declare God's word in its fullness may take comfort from God letting none of Samuel's words fall to the ground. The same God has promised that his word will not return to him void (Isaiah 55:10–11).

FOR FURTHER STUDY

1. *1 Kings 22:1–28 provides another example of a prophet who had to declare an unpleasant message to one in authority. Identify the prophet and summarize his message. Look at the contrast between the attitudes of the king of Israel and the king of Judah towards the word of God.*

2. *Read Jeremiah 36:20–32. What did King Jehoiakim do with the word of God? How did the Lord respond to Jehoiakim's act?*

TO THINK ABOUT AND DISCUSS

1. *What can we do to hear the word of God faithfully? How should we listen to it? What should our attitude be to it when it is preached? Think about the practical steps we can take to help ourselves be ready to hear it and respond to it.*

2. *How should God's people respond when a preacher declares unpleasant truth? What things do we not enjoy hearing a preacher declare to us? How should we respond to preaching we find difficult to accept? What are the dangers if we ignore such preaching?*

Notes

1 **John Trapp,** *Commentary on the Old & New Testaments* (Eureka, California: Tanski Publications, 1997), vol. i, p. 418.

5 Conspicuous by absence

1 Samuel 4:1–22

Chapters 4 through 6 of 1 Samuel describe one of the darkest, foulest eras in the history of the nation of Israel. It was an era of defeat and humiliation for the people of God, an era in which they were oppressed by the Philistines and were deprived of the visible representation of their covenant with God.

It should not escape our notice that Samuel is conspicuously absent from these chapters. The only mention of him is in the first sentence of this section, a sentence that should undoubtedly have been included in the closing verses of chapter 3.

God had chosen Samuel to be his instrument in the work of spiritual renewal, but after an initial receptiveness to his ministry (3:19–21), the elders of the nation evidently tuned him out. They apparently did not consult him when they decided to go to war against the Philistines. He was most certainly not consulted after Israel suffered an initial defeat and the decision was made to carry the ark of God into battle. Alexander Maclaren is correct in saying: 'Probably Samuel's mission made an unwholesome ferment in minds which were quite untouched by its highest significance, and so led to a precipitate rebellion.'[1]

When we encounter Samuel again, we find him saying to the nation: 'If you return to the LORD with all your hearts ... he will deliver you from the hand of the Philistines' (7:3).

If only that message had been heard and heeded at the beginning of chapter 4, many lives could have been spared and much heartache avoided.

All of this should convince us that true revival often comes very slowly and with fits and starts. The preaching and teaching of the word of God is like planting a seed, and, as everyone knows, there is a good bit of time between planting and harvesting.

NOT PRESENT TO ANSWER A VITAL QUESTION

What a disaster Israel experienced on this occasion! She went out to engage the Philistines in battle and lost 4000 men.

Who was responsible for this terrible defeat? Verse 2 tells us that the Philistines defeated Israel, but in verse 3 the elders of Israel attribute their defeat to God. Which was it? Did the Philistines defeat Israel? Or did God do it? Or should we say that Israel defeated Israel? The answer is 'all of the above'.

We cannot understand this apart from Israel's covenant relationship with God. One aspect of this covenant was his guarantee that Israel would be victorious over their enemies in warfare if they lived in obedience to his commands. Moses put it this way: 'But it shall come to pass, if you do not obey the voice of the LORD your God, to observe carefully all his commandments ... the LORD will cause you to be defeated before your enemies' (Deuteronomy 28:15,25).

In light of this we can say that the defeat of Israel was due to the Lord using the Philistines to crush Israel as a punishment for her sins.

After losing 4000 men, the elders of Israel came together for an emergency meeting. They wasted no time getting to the heart of the matter: 'Why has the LORD defeated us today before the Philistines?' (v. 3).

That was certainly the right question for them to ask. They knew the Philistines could not have defeated them if the Lord had been with them. But it was obvious that the Lord had left them to themselves.

The next thing we expect to read is that these elders initiated a search for Samuel so he could declare to them and the nation the teachings of Moses in Deuteronomy and call them to repentance. That would have been the right answer to the right question.

But they did no such thing. After raising the right question, they came up with the wrong answer! They instead concluded that God had not given them the victory because they had failed to carry the ark of the covenant into battle.

This answer completely ignored the fact that the ark was not to be moved from the tabernacle (Deuteronomy 12:5,11). The high priest was the only one who was to see the ark! It was housed in the Most Holy Place into which he entered once a year to make atonement for the sins of the people by sprinkling blood on the mercy seat of the ark. But people who ignore the word of God at so many points are not troubled by ignoring it at yet another.

Their answer also misconstrued the purpose of the ark. It was a symbol, and the reality it symbolized was far greater than the ark itself. It was a visible representation of the presence of God, but it did not guarantee God's presence and power. The symbols God employed in his covenant with Israel only had value if they were combined with true faith in the hearts of his people. S.G. DeGraaf writes: 'The ark was certainly the sign of the presence of the Lord, but the Lord revealed and gave himself in that sign only to a people who looked to him in faith.'[2]

It was ironic that the ark contained the two tablets of stone on which God had written the Ten Commandments, the keeping of which would have assured them of victory over the Philistines. The presence of those broken commandments on the battlefield only served to give mute testimony to the enormity of their sins and drove God farther away. Joseph Hall observes: 'Those who regarded not the God of the ark think themselves safe and happy in the ark of God.'[3]

When the ark of God arrived on the scene, the Israelite soldiers greeted it with a tremendous outburst of emotion, which sparked no small amount of consternation among the Philistines. But when the fighting resumed, the ark and the emotion were of no value, and Israel was soundly trounced (v. 10).

NOT PRESENT TO PREVENT A TERRIBLE BLUNDER

Hophni and Phinehas, the sons of Eli, brought the ark to the battlefield. After all, the law of God required that it be carried only by priests (Deuteronomy 31:24–25)! Isn't it astonishing how scrupulous people can be about one detail after ignoring a thousand!

Had it not been for this decision to bring the ark into battle,

Hophni and Phinehas would have been safe at Shiloh. Had they been the priests they should have been, they would never have agreed with this hare-brained scheme.

But the hand of the Lord was at work in all these things. Little did Hophni and Phinehas realize that, as they strode along with the ark, they were marching towards death. The Lord had promised that they would both die on the same day, but it was fitting that these men who had so violently disregarded his law should die violently and that these who had lived as pagans should die at the hands of pagans.

It was a day of grim despair. As the word filtered through the nation of Israel, the people reeled at the magnitude of what had happened. Their army had sustained staggering losses, their sacred ark had been seized and carried off as a spoil of war, and Eli had died when, from the shock of the sweeping defeat, he fell from a stool and broke his neck.

Eli's daughter-in-law, the wife of Phinehas, best summarized the dismay that rolled across Israel. Immediately after giving birth to a son, she died with the sombre instruction to name him 'Ichabod', which meant 'inglorious'. Why such a melancholy name? The dying mother explained it in these words: 'The glory has departed from Israel' (4:21).

But she was not correct, as H.L. Ellison explains: 'The glory of God had indeed departed, but not because the ark of God had been captured; the ark had been captured because the glory had already departed.'[4]

THE IMPORTANCE OF BELIEVING AND OBEYING GOD

Part of God's covenant with Israel was his promise to bring judgement on Israel for disobeying his commands. We do well to remember that the Lord has made certain promises to us as well. He has promised that all who reject the perfect salvation he has provided in Christ will most definitely perish in eternity. Such a promise seems far-fetched to the sceptical minds of this day. But Scripture is filled with instances of God fulfilling promises that appeared to be unlikely and improbable, and we may rest assured that he will fulfil this promise as well.

Happily, there is another promise on which we may depend. It is God's promise to forgive all those who see their sins, mourn over them and turn from them to embrace the salvation of Christ Jesus.

We also do well to remember that God's commandments have not been withdrawn or cancelled. They are still in force. And when God's people play fast and loose with those commands, they invite disaster into their lives just as Israel did when she went out against the Philistines.

THE FOLLY OF TRYING TO USE GOD

It is easy enough for us to see the folly of the Israelites, but do we see our own? We also can be guilty of ignoring God's commands and then seeking to press him into service when a crisis looms. We can persuade ourselves that the outer representations of faith assure us of his presence. We can seek to manufacture emotion in our worship services, assuming that mere emotion will secure God's presence. Dale Ralph Davis writes: 'Whenever the church stops confessing "Thou art worthy" and begins chanting "Thou art useful"—well, then you know the ark of God has been captured again.'[5]

We do not like the God who commands and requires obedience. We much prefer the useful God—the one who does things for us. Are you sick? Are you troubled? Are you hard pressed financially? Just fire off a prayer, and God will come running! And if he doesn't, it is because we have failed in faith.

God is, of course, committed to doing good for his people, but here is the rub: he does not always agree with us on what constitutes our good. When Israel was thrashed by the Philistines, it did not appear that God had done good for her. But think about it. Through this defeat, the Lord removed from Israel's leadership the godless Hophni and Phinehas and the ineffective Eli. And he humbled Israel. All of this was for their good.

But was not God himself humiliated in this defeat? Here is an amazing thing! God is willing to endure humiliation for the good of his people. That is, after all, what the cross is about. There God endured the humiliation of our sins to grant his people the good of eternal life.

For further study ▶

FOR FURTHER STUDY

1. *Study Exodus 25:10–22. Write a description of the ark of the covenant.*

2. *Read Leviticus 26:1–17 and Deuteronomy 28:1–25. What was necessary for Israel to defeat her enemies?*

TO THINK ABOUT AND DISCUSS

1. *In what ways do we try to use God? Think of both some subtle and more blatant examples. How might you encourage your children or other members of your family and friends to understand and obey this principle more consistently?*

2. *What do you think it means for God's glory to depart from his people? How would it show in the life of our churches if God's glory were to depart from us today? How should we respond to this possibility?*

Notes

1 **Alexander Maclaren,** *Expositions of Holy Scripture* (Grand Rapids: Baker Book House, 1974), vol. ii, p. 276.

2 **S.G. DeGraaf,** *Promise and Deliverance* (Presbyterian and Reformed Publishing Co., 1978), vol. ii, pp. 73–4.

3 Cited by **Maclaren,** p. 278.

4 Cited by **Davis,** *Looking on the Heart: 1 Samuel 1–14* (Grand Rapids: Baker Book House, 1994), p. 55.

5 **Davis,** p. 53.

6 Lightness and heaviness

1 Samuel 5:1–7:1

The Philistines were feeling quite upbeat. Their soldiers had been terrified when they heard that the ark of God had arrived on the battlefield. But after their initial dismay, those soldiers became more determined, won the battle and captured the ark.

Their victory must have brought euphoria to the whole nation. As far as the Philistines were concerned, this triumph signalled the end of their hated enemy. Israel had, as it were, pulled out all the stops. She had played her ace in bringing the ark of the covenant to the battlefield, but even that had not kept her from going down in humiliating defeat.

THE LIGHTNESS OF DAGON

The Philistines had to see their victory as proof that the God of Israel was not as powerful as they had been led to believe. Their god, Dagon, was far superior! Since Dagon had supposedly won the victory over Israel's God, it was only fitting that they should place the ark in his temple.

Their euphoria did not last long. We might say they got raided by the lost ark! They thought they had defeated the God of Israel, but they were in for the proverbial 'rude awakening'.

When they went to the temple of Dagon the next morning, they found that their god had toppled from his stand.

How embarrassing! The first night the conquered God is in the house of the conquering god, and the latter falls flat on his face! And the way in which he fell was particularly embarrassing—face down before the ark of God, as if he were paying homage to it (5:3)!

Such a thing would seem to be enough to cause even these hardened Philistines to think, but they quickly dismissed any thought that begged to lodge in their minds and promptly seized their god and set him back in his place (5:3). Imagine worshipping a god who had to be helped up!

The following morning was to prove even more embarrassing. When the Philistines arrived in Dagon's temple, they were distressed to find he had again fallen prostrate before the ark, and this time his head and his hands were broken off (5:4). The seemingly conquered God of Israel had not been conquered at all.

Instead of acknowledging this, the Philistines proceeded to declare the place where Dagon's head had fallen a holy place, and they made a rule that no one should step on it (5:5)!

THE HEAVINESS OF GOD

'Diving Dagon' should have been enough to convince the Philistines that they were on the wrong track, but God had not finished pouring evidence on them. The account emphasizes that his hand was heavy upon them (5:6,9,11; 6:5). They soon began to break out in huge, painful boils (5:6).

They simply ignored Dagon's two falls, but boils are mighty hard to ignore. This newest problem wrung the admission from them that the God of Israel was indeed at work in their midst

(5:7), but their response to this was to send the ark away to their neighbouring province (5:8).

The hand of God that came down so heavily on the Philistines did the same upon the residents of the Israelite village of Beth Shemesh. These people should have known better! They 'looked into the ark of the LORD', and God 'struck' them, killing seventy (6:19). (The phrase 'fifty thousand and seventy men of the people' probably means 'seventy men of whom fifty were elders over thousands'.)

The sin of these people was that of gross familiarity, which caused them to treat the ark as a curiosity to be gaped and gawked at. It was, rather, an emblem of God's covenant of salvation with his people and was therefore to be treated with reverence.

THINK ABOUT THE GOD WHO CANNOT BE DEFEATED

We have false gods aplenty today. They are not as patently silly and foolish as a half-human and half-fish as Dagon was, but our gods are no less false because they are sophisticated.

Just as the Philistines of that ancient day were eager to sound the death knell of the nation of Israel and the God of Israel, so the devotees of these modern-day false gods are eager to do the same with Christianity and God. And it oftentimes appears that Christianity is indeed on her last leg and that her God has been conquered.

But many who have been quick to trumpet the death of Christianity have found the reports of her demise to be premature. Voltaire, the French philosopher who died in 1778, said Christianity would become extinct within one hundred years. It is a delicious irony that the Geneva Bible Society used his press and his house to publish scores of Bibles only fifty years after his death.[1]

Another example of this very thing is the edict of Roman emperor Diocletian in AD 303 that called for the destruction of Christians and the Bible. Twenty-five years later Diocletian's successor, Constantine, commissioned Eusebius to prepare fifty Bibles at the government's expense.[2]

Yet another example is the prevailing attitude toward Christianity in England in the early 1700s. Bishop Joseph Butler observed that scepticism had become so widespread that Christianity was treated as though 'it was now discovered to be fictitious ... and nothing remained but to set it up as the subject of mirth and ridicule'.[3] But Christianity rose from that low ebb to spectacular vitality through the ministries of George Whitefield and John and Charles Wesley.

These episodes and many like them led Bernard Ramm to observe: 'A thousand times over, the death knell of the Bible has been sounded, the funeral procession formed, the inscription cut on the tombstone, and the committal read. But somehow the corpse never stays put.'[4]

How these things should encourage and hearten every believer in Jesus Christ! No matter how bleak the times, no matter how wolfish the devil's wolves and sheepish the Lord's sheep, God's cause is ultimately going to triumph.

THINK ABOUT THE EVIDENCE FOR GOD

A second lesson for us to draw from this passage is that the God who cannot be defeated is also the God who has given more than sufficient evidence to win us over.

After Dagon took his second tumble we might expect to read

that one Philistine said: 'That's enough. We cannot go on believing in a god that can't even stand up. Somebody back a chariot to the door and get this joker out of here.' And we might then expect to read that another said: 'The fact Dagon never fell before we brought the Israelites' ark in here indicates that their God is greater than ours even though we won the battle.' And then we might expect to read that still another said: 'I think we should investigate their God more fully.'

But, incredibly enough, no one said any of those things. The Philistines saw indisputable evidence that their god was false, and compelling evidence that the God of Israel was the true God; yet they decided to set their god up again and keep right on worshipping him.

These Philistines may seem very dense to us, but the sad truth is that many, without realizing it, are caught in the Philistine syndrome. This syndrome consists of ignoring the evidence, and when it can no longer be ignored, trying to stay completely away from it.

The evidence continues to pour in that the false gods of our own day are not working. They have neither the wisdom nor the power to deal with man's fundamental need of a new heart, but most of their followers adamantly refuse to face up to their failure. Even as the evidence pours in, these followers go on about the business of 'god-propping'. For example, evidence abounds that we are not basically good at heart and cannot be educated into good behaviour. But the 'god-proppers' continue to insist that just a little more education will finally make us into dazzling specimens of morality and virtue. Education is vital, of course, but it has yet to change a sinner into a saint. Only the Spirit of God can do that.

On top of the evidence of failed gods is the evidence for the truth of Christianity. In comparison to the evidence we have for this truth, the evidence the Philistines saw may be likened to a dim beam from a tiny penlight on a foggy night.

What is this evidence for the truth of Christianity? There is fulfilled prophecy. There is that supreme evidence, the resurrection of Jesus Christ. There is the amazing survival of the Christian church despite numerous efforts to wipe it from the face of the earth. There are the testimonies of multitudes to the transforming power of Jesus Christ. There are the daily confirmations in our society of the truth of the Bible's moral principles.

What is our response to the failures of the gods of today? What is our response to all the evidence for Christianity? We can, like the Philistines of old, ignore these pieces of evidence or try to send them away. We can send Christian witnesses away, and we can stay away from the churches where the evidence is preached and taught. Or by the grace and power of God, we can break the Philistine syndrome and accept the evidence. The one thing we cannot do is successfully fight against God. We can claim victory over him, but we can never defeat him. We can run from him, but we can never escape him.

The course of wisdom, therefore, is to throw down our arms and stop our running. We can listen carefully to what the almighty God has to say about our sinful condition and about the eternal condemnation that awaits all sinners. We can listen gladly to what he says about a perfect salvation that delivers from sin and judgement, a salvation that is available through the Lord Jesus Christ.

THINK ABOUT STANDING BEFORE GOD

We have to say that the residents of Beth Shemesh got the point. After their casual familiarity with the ark led to severe judgement, they asked: 'Who is able to stand before this holy LORD God?' (6:20).

God is holy! And he has made it clear that only holy people can stand in his holy presence. That means that we have an enormous problem. Here is God demanding holiness, and here we are in our sins. Indeed, how can unholy people stand before the holy God?

The answer to this is, of course, that they can do so only through Christ. He lived the righteous life that we have failed to live. He has the holiness that God demands, and that holiness is imparted to all who receive him as their Lord and Saviour.

THINK ABOUT GOD SUSTAINING HIS OWN CAUSE

Isn't it fascinating that God did not need any help in bringing the ark back to Israel?

We have a tendency to think that God needs our help, but he doesn't. It is our immense privilege that God uses us as instruments to achieve his will, but he doesn't need us. To those who think that God needs us to uphold his honour by taking away the scandal of the cross, let the word go out—he doesn't need our help!

For further study ▶

FOR FURTHER STUDY

1. *Read 1 Kings 18:1–40. Name the god who is discredited in this passage. How did this take place? How was God vindicated?*
2. *Look up 2 Samuel 6:1–7. What act of overfamiliarity with God is found here? What were the consequences of this?*

TO THINK ABOUT AND DISCUSS

1. *What do you consider to be the most persuasive piece of evidence for Christianity? Give reasons. Are there ways in which we can use such evidence for evangelistic purposes, to persuade others of the truth of Christianity?*
2. *In what ways are Christians showing overfamiliarity with God today? Think about our church services, and our personal walk with God. How can we maintain a right reverence for God?*

Notes

1 **Josh McDowell,** *Evidence That Demands a Verdict* (Campus Crusade for Christ, Inc., 1999), p. 10.

2 **McDowell,** p. 10.

3 **Arnold A. Dallimore,** *George Whitefield: The Life and Times of the Great Evangelist of the Eighteenth-Century Revival* (London: Banner of Truth, 1970), vol. i, p. 31.

4 **McDowell,** p. 10.

7 Samuel, front and centre

1 Samuel 7:2–17

Although the ark of God was back in Israel, true religious vitality did not accompany it. Gordon Keddie summarizes those twenty years in these words: 'Israel languished under the oppression of the Philistines and the depression of spiritual declension. The tabernacle struggled on under the descendants of Eli but the fact that the ark sat, inactive, year after year, in the house of Abinadab only served to emphasise how far the people of God had fallen.'[1]

Suddenly a bright ray of hope pierces the gloom: 'And all the house of Israel lamented after the LORD' (v. 2).

SAMUEL LEADS HIS PEOPLE TO RENEWAL

How are we to explain this lamenting? The next phrase gives us the answer: 'Then Samuel spoke to all the house of Israel' (v. 3). After his long absence, Samuel is back!

The truth is that Samuel had never been absent from Israel. We may be sure that he was quietly and doggedly working to spread the word of God even though there is no mention of him in chapters 4 through 6.

Now that quiet ministry begins to bear fruit. Gordon Keddie

writes: 'Trouble concentrated their minds and, bit by bit, they came to see that God was their only hope. The ministry of Samuel during these years would have had its leavening effect in bringing this national spiritual crisis to the boil.'[2]

The people of Israel finally came to see their desperate condition. They recognized at long last that their problems were all due to the fact that they had driven the Lord away because of their sins, and they began to yearn for him again. It should go without saying that it is impossible to yearn for God without yearning for his word. This is where Samuel comes in.

PUTTING AWAY
Samuel emphasized that there could be no true revival as long as the people continued to hold on to idols. The Ashtoreths mentioned in this passage (v. 3) were particularly lewd representations of Canaanite goddesses.

The people demonstrated their seriousness and sincerity about revival by doing as Samuel demanded (v. 4).

COMING TOGETHER
The work of revival in verses 1 through 4 was probably done on a village by village level as Samuel travelled the length and breadth of the nation. But when the work progressed to a certain point, Samuel realized that it was time to call the whole nation together for a solemn assembly (vv. 5–6). This happened at Mizpah.

POURING OUT
When the people came together for the assembly, Samuel drew water and 'poured it out before the LORD' (v. 6). This was a

visible and open display of what was going on in their hearts. By doing this, Samuel was picturing the pouring out of their hearts in true repentance before God.

Another indication of their repentance was fasting (v. 6). Food lost its appeal to them because they were lost in the larger concern of getting right with God.

This pouring-out of their hearts before God in true repentance led to a pouring-out of public confession as the people cried out: 'We have sinned against the LORD' (v. 6).

SAMUEL LEADS HIS PEOPLE AGAINST THE PHILISTINES

No sooner had the children of Israel experienced genuine revival than the Philistines began to prepare to engage them in battle (v. 7).

Satan is interested in God's people being cold, indifferent and sinful. It is not surprising, therefore, that he always stirs up his people in opposition when God stirs up his people in revival.

How different was the attitude of the people on this occasion! Here they do not assume, as they had twenty years earlier, that God would fight for them regardless of the condition of their hearts. Instead they cry out to Samuel to pray for them. They realize that they are not worthy of God's blessing, and they cast themselves totally upon God and his grace. Samuel symbolized their wholehearted devotion to the Lord by offering a burnt sacrifice.

They were in and of themselves no match for the Philistines, but their God was more than sufficient. He caused the heavens to rumble with such thunder that the Philistines were completely disorientated and easily defeated. So Israel experienced victory on the same battlefield on which they had been defeated twenty years earlier. As a result the people of Israel were able to reclaim lost territory (v. 14) and to enjoy a period of peace and tranquillity (vv. 13, 15–17).

After the battle was over, Samuel led the people in a solemn ceremony of thanksgiving. He set up a stone and called it 'Ebenezer', which means 'up to this point the Lord has helped us'. Through this ceremony the people testified to their awareness that they owed the victory to the Lord, and they also confessed their need for his ongoing help. He had helped them to this point, but they now knew their sinful inclinations were such that they would continue to need his help.

DON'T GIVE UP ON REVIVAL

True revival is possible even in the darkest of times. Many argue otherwise. Some rule out any possibility of revival on prophetic grounds. They believe God intends for things to grow progressively worse so the Lord Jesus can come and the Antichrist can be revealed. Revival would 'gum up' the plan! Some rule revival out on sociological grounds. They argue that revival was a phenomenon that flourished in less advanced times, and, now that times have changed, it can no longer be expected. Some argue against it on practical grounds. The times are too hard, apathy is too strong, evil is too entrenched. Such realities render talk of revival a waste of time.

The experience of Israel under Samuel shows us that it is always too early to give up on God. Nothing is impossible with him, and he has not taught anything in his word—prophetically or otherwise—that justifies apathy and carelessness about spiritual things.

SEEK REVIVAL

The experience of Israel under Samuel provides an agenda for all who long to see God revive his people. We must admit that revival is always the prerogative of a sovereign God. We cannot set it up or produce it. But we can and should give ourselves to coming together with other believers to seek the Lord, put away our idols and pour out our hearts in true repentance.

Serious and devoted attention to these matters will in and of itself be evidence that the sovereign God has already been pleased to begin his work of revival within us.

ERECT AN EBENEZER

In setting up a stone and calling it 'Ebenezer' (v. 12), Samuel provides a spiritual principle for the people of God in every era, namely, to believe that God will work on our behalf in the future because of the undoubted instances in which he has done so in the past.

John Newton made use of this principle in his hymn 'Begone, unbelief':

> His love in time past forbids me to think
> He'll leave me at last in trouble to sink;
> Each sweet Ebenezer I have in review
> Confirms his good pleasure to help me quite through.

The Lord's Supper serves as the grandest of all Ebenezers. As the people of God come to the Lord's Table, they recall his redeeming death on their behalf. And as they contemplate that death, they find strength for the trials they are facing and the burdens they are carrying. Those trials and burdens may be of such a nature that it appears as if God has forsaken them. But the Ebenezer of the Lord's Supper drills this logic into the hearts of each believer: If God did for me in the cross of his Son the greatest of all things, I must not think for a moment that he will refuse to do for me a lesser thing, namely, stay with me as I face this trial and carry this burden.

FOR FURTHER STUDY

1. Read 2 Chronicles 7:14. To whom does God speak? What does he call them to do and what does he promise?
2. 2 Chronicles 20:1–30 describes another battle in which God gave his people victory. What preceded this battle?

TO THINK ABOUT AND DISCUSS

1. Examine your life. What are some things that you need to be 'putting away'? Are there things that we as churches need to 'put away' as well—in our practices or attitudes?
2. What can you do to encourage other Christians to come together to seek revival? What practical things can we do to seek revival?

Notes

1 **Gordon Keddie,** *The Dawn of a Kingdom* (Darlington: Evangelical Press, 1988), p. 80.
2 **Keddie,** p. 80.

8 Keeping up with the times

1 Samuel 8:1–22

Whentheпeople of Israel refused to be governed by the word of God, they were soundly defeated by the Philistines, and they lost the ark of the covenant. But when they saw the error of their ways and began seriously to heed Samuel's preaching, they conquered the Philistines, recovered lost territory and enjoyed an era of peace and tranquillity.

It would seem, therefore, that the national motto of Israel would have been: 'Obey the Lord'. We might even expect to read that Israel had learned from experience and that they continued to live in obedience to the Lord and 'lived happily ever after'.

But that was not the case. We cannot say how long the people enjoyed the benefits of the revival described in chapter 7. It could have been a period of several years. But we do not get far into chapter 8 before we realize that it had come to an end.

THE ELDERS SPEAK TO SAMUEL

A new spirit was at work in Israel, evidenced by the demand the elders placed upon Samuel: 'Now make us a king to judge us like all the nations' (v. 5).

It all sounds so innocent. What could possibly be wrong with the people wanting a king?

The elders presented Samuel with reasons that sounded plausible. His sons, whom he had evidently appointed to share his responsibilities and to be his successors, were nothing at all like him. The elders did not want such poor specimens ruling the nation, and it had begun to look as if they would soon be doing exactly that as Samuel was growing old and feeble.

The time seemed right for a change. What better way to ease Samuel's sons out of the picture than to send a committee to explain that their services were no longer needed because the nation was going down the king route?

When we become infatuated with a particular course of action, it isn't hard to manufacture justification for it. A king would both take Samuel's sons out of the picture and bring Israel into step with the other nations. Israel had been behind the times. While other nations had kings, she had been under the leadership of various judges. This style of leadership, effective as it often had been, was now outmoded. It was a new day, a day that called for Israel to take her place as an equal among the family of nations.

As far as these elders were concerned, the very thing they were doing at that moment was proof of their point. When a neighbouring nation had a crisis to discuss, the king called his advisors to his palace. Here they were, though, talking to their leader in a little hut in the village of Ramah (v. 4). How could they expect to have the respect of other nations when their leader wore the common attire of a prophet and lived in a hut?

They had discussed it among themselves, and they agreed it made perfect sense. They had the feeling that Samuel would be opposed, but they were prepared to throw down the gauntlet. They would simply tell him this was the way things had to be.

In all their consultations, there is no mention of anyone seeking God or hearing from God. Had they done so, things would have been very different. Had they looked into his word, they would have discovered that God did not want Israel to be like all the other nations. He had put Israel on a pedestal, and she would have to step down to be like everyone else (Deuteronomy 7:6–8; 28:9–10).

Had they bothered to consult God, they would have found that he did not want a king for Israel. It was not that he never intended for Israel to have a king. The law of Moses clearly assumes that a king was very much in God's plan for the nation (Deuteronomy 17:14–20). It was rather that God had his own time for doing this.

Why did God not want a king at this particular time? The account does not say. God owes us no explanations. He is infinite in wisdom. He makes no mistakes. All we need to know is what he wants. Why he wants it is beside the point.

Furthermore, had the elders of Israel consulted God on the matter, they would have discovered that there was no need to fear the future. They only needed to concern themselves with living in obedience to God, and he would take care of everything else. He had taken care of Hophni and Phinehas, and he would have no difficulty in doing the same with the sons of Samuel.

THE LORD SPEAKS TO SAMUEL

Samuel's obvious displeasure should have been enough to derail the plan (v. 6). It should have been enough to make one of these elders come to his senses and speak along these lines: 'Brethren, we would do well to drop this idea. Remember the past. When we refused to listen to Samuel, we had nothing but trouble. And when we did listen, we had nothing but blessing. I suggest we shelve this nutty scheme indefinitely.'

Ever the man of prayer, Samuel took the request of the elders to the Lord (v. 6), and the Lord told him to give them a king. In making this request, they were thumbing their noses in the face of God, and they must once again learn by bitter experience their folly.

In allowing them to have a king, the Lord also gave them the opportunity to rethink and repent. Samuel would state in no uncertain terms the unpleasant aspects of kingship (v. 9).

SAMUEL SPEAKS TO THE ELDERS

Samuel laid it all out. He held nothing back. Their king would make life difficult for them. Their sons and daughters would be conscripted to serve him, and the load of taxation would be heavy and oppressive. And the very ones who were crying for a king would 'cry out' because of their king (v. 18).

Samuel could not close his sombre message without putting the issue in bald, stark terms. The king who caused them such heartache would be the one whom they had chosen for themselves (v. 18). He would be their king, not God's. And the God whom they spurned would refuse to hear them when they cried out in anguish (v. 18).

The portrayal of such a grim scenario would seem to have been more than enough to get the elders to change their minds, but they did no such thing: 'Nevertheless the people refused to obey the voice of Samuel' (v. 19).

They became even more adamant. They began by saying: 'Now make us a king' (v. 5) and 'Give us a king' (v. 6), but now they are saying: 'We will have a king' (v. 19).

The voice of Samuel was, of course, the voice of the Lord (v. 10). So these people had a plain word from God, and they deliberately scorned it. The enormity of their sin is breathtaking!

KEEPING UP WITH THE TRUTH OR KEEPING UP WITH THE TIMES?

Believers today can give into the 'king thing' quite as much as the elders of Samuel's time. We do so every time we set aside the truth of God in order to make the church more relevant.

Many Christian leaders hold their Bibles in one hand and the latest opinion poll in the other. But they read the poll first and then their Bibles. And much concerned to prevent Christianity from being thought out of date, they begin to modify and adjust the message of the Bible to fit the times.

The Bible contains a straightforward message about the guilt of our sin and the holy nature of God that requires him to pronounce judgement on sin. It also plainly proclaims the judgement that he has pronounced, namely, eternal separation from himself.

The same Bible also declares God's gracious provision of forgiveness for sinners. That provision is the redeeming death of his Son, Jesus Christ, on the cross. That death consisted of Jesus receiving the wrath of God in the place of sinners. All who repent of their sins and entrust themselves to what Jesus did on that cross realize this glorious truth: If Jesus received the wrath of God on the cross, there is no wrath left for them to receive. God only demands that the penalty for sin be paid once, and if Jesus paid it, there is nothing left for believing sinners to pay.

But these great themes—sin, wrath and blood—are deemed by many to be 'turn-offs'. Something more 'user-friendly' is needed! And the 'king thing' takes place again!

GOD BLESSING OR DISCIPLINING?

The desire of the elders for a king also reminds us that answered prayer is not necessarily a blessing. God's discipline of his disobedient children is a real thing (Hebrews 12:5–11). That discipline can take different forms. Sometimes God brings adversity, and sometimes he withholds blessings. But he can also, as he did with the elders of Israel, let his people have what they want so they will learn to want better in the future!

God's discipline, whatever form it takes, is never a matter of God being hateful and cruel. It always flows from a heart of love and is designed to help his children.

FOR FURTHER STUDY

1. *Jeremiah 42:1–43:7 provides another example of people who refused to listen to the word of God. What was the issue in these verses?*

2. *Read Hosea 13:9–11. What is the Lord's explanation for giving Israel a king?*

TO THINK ABOUT AND DISCUSS

1. *What indications do you see that the church today is trying to keep up with the times without being guided by the Bible? Think of the message being preached; the style and form of worship; the songs we sing, etc.*

2. *God disciplines his people in various ways—sometimes even by letting them have what they want! What are the ways in which you think you have experienced the Lord's discipline? How can we tell whether answered prayer is a blessing or part of God's discipline? What effect should this have on our praying?*

9 The privileges of Saul

1 Samuel 9:1–11:15

'Saul' is one of Scripture's most stained names. It's right there with Cain, Esau, Lot, Achan and Joash. Men with enormous potential and numerous privileges! Men united in infamy because they squandered all!

Saul was given tremendous privileges and wondrous opportunities, but he lived beneath the former and missed the latter. He was a failure!

We tend to make excuses for failures. They were not given the proper upbringing! They were products of a bad environment! But there was no excuse for Saul. His failure was due to refusing to obey the commandments of the Lord. He came to the throne of Israel fortified with certain things that he should have used to shield himself from disobedience, but he left himself open to failure.

A CRASH COURSE

The chapters before us indicate that Saul was in need of a crash course on submitting to the Lord. He was hardly a spiritual giant at this time in his life. Although Samuel had been travelling the length and breadth of Israel for many years, Saul's servant knew much more about Samuel than Saul did. And the servant appears to have regarded Samuel as some sort of magician whose primary purpose was to help locate lost items! It was on that basis that Saul agreed to see Samuel. That Saul-like spirit which is only interested in religion providing temporal benefits is still alive and well today!

We can safely assume that Saul was not with Samuel very long before he learned the importance of a vibrant spirituality that manifests itself in obedience to the Lord. It could very well be that a good portion of Samuel's 'roof-top discourse' was devoted to this matter (9:25).

If we had been there, we would undoubtedly have heard Samuel share with Saul the words of Moses regarding the role of the king of Israel:

> Also it shall be, when he sits on the throne of his kingdom, that he shall write for himself a copy of this law in a book .... And it shall be with him, and he shall read it all the days of his life, that he may learn to fear the LORD his God and be careful to observe all the words of this law and these statutes ... that he may not turn aside from the commandment to the right hand or to the left, and that he may prolong his days in his kingdom, he and his children in the midst of Israel
>
> (Deuteronomy 17:18–20).

The main qualification for being king of Israel, then, was to understand that the position did not entail absolute authority. There was another king. God was the King in heaven, and Saul was to be the 'under-king' on earth. It was the job of the king on earth to recognize the authority of the King in heaven, to obey his will and to lead the people to do the same.

UNMISTAKABLE SIGNS

It is also safe to say that Saul came to the throne with signs that served as powerful incentives for obeying the Lord.

SIGNS OF THE AUTHORITY OF GOD

First, he was given one astounding demonstration after another of the sovereign authority of the Lord over all things.

Look at the incredible chain of events that led Saul to Samuel, and, through Samuel, to the throne of Israel. It all began with his father's straying donkeys (9:3–4). Saul and his servant set out to find them, but this proved to be no easy task. Through the mountains of Ephraim, the land of Shalisha, the land of Shaalim and the land of the Benjamites, the search was conducted without success.

When they reached the land of Zuph, Saul decided the enterprise was hopeless and was ready to call it off (9:5). That's when the servant realized they were near Samuel's home town of Ramah (the word 'Ramah' means 'this town'—see 9:6). Perhaps Samuel could tell them where to find the donkeys!

Saul rejected the idea because he had nothing with which to pay Samuel for his services. But the servant just happened to have a coin!

They then asked some young ladies if they had seen Samuel, and it just happened that Samuel was passing by (9:12)!

Let's see now. Donkeys just happened to get lost. The search just happened to lead to where Samuel was. The servant just happened to know about Samuel and also just happened to have a coin. And Samuel just happened to be in town and even passing by as Saul and his servant were asking about him. That is a lot of 'just happened's!

When Saul learned that he was to be king of Israel, he must have reflected long and hard on how he searched for donkeys and found his destiny. And he must have realized that this was not mere coincidence but the hand of God. He must also have realized that a God who can exercise such minute control over human events is to be feared and obeyed.

SIGNS OF THE RELIABILITY OF GOD'S WORD

In addition to this demonstration of the authority of God, Saul was given several powerful indications of the reliability of God's word.

The morning after Saul learned he was to be the king of Israel, Samuel gave him three distinct prophecies. First, he, Saul, would meet two men at Rachel's tomb who would report to him that the donkeys had been found and that his father had begun to worry about him (10:2).

Then Saul would meet three men at the terebinth tree of Tabor who would give him two loaves of bread (10:4).

Finally, Saul would meet a group of prophets who would be prophesying, and the Spirit of God would come so mightily upon him that he would join in the prophesying (10:5–6).

Each prophecy was distinct and detailed. In the first two prophecies, Samuel gave specific numbers of men whom Saul would meet. In the last two, he described what they would be carrying. And he gave precise locations in all three.

The succinct comment of Scripture on these three prophecies is this: 'All those signs came to pass that day' (10:9).

What effect did these fulfilled prophecies have on Saul? Any right-thinking person would have marvelled at the precise fulfilment of them and would surely have concluded that God's word is true down to the very last detail. If it is true in all it says, the course of wisdom is to obey it!

A final incentive Saul received for obeying God's word was what we might call the public confirmation of the private announcement. Samuel announced to Saul privately that he was to be the king of Israel. A few days later Samuel called the people of Israel together to select their king (10:17). The selection was to be made by casting lots. It would seem to be a matter of sheer luck for Saul to be chosen, but the lot fell first on his tribe, then on his family, and finally on him. That which Samuel had spoken privately had been confirmed.

When Saul contemplated this, it had to occur to him that God is sovereign and his word is infallibly true, and that his job as king was to obey this God just as the words of Moses so plainly taught.

A SOLEMN WARNING

On the same morning on which Samuel gave Saul the three prophecies, he spoke of a coming day when it would be necessary for Saul to wait for him for seven days at Gilgal (10:8).

It was as if Samuel was saying: 'Saul, you are going to be given abundant proofs that God's word is true and must be trusted, but you cannot succeed as king until you prove that you are willing to trust that word, come what may.'

That test probably sounded easy to Saul when Samuel announced it. I can hear him saying: 'Wait at Gilgal for seven days until Samuel arrives! What is so hard about that?' But when the time came for the doing of it, Saul found it to be so very difficult that he failed.

ONGOING INCENTIVES

Lots of things have changed since that ancient day. Kings and kingdoms have passed away. Other things have not changed. The importance of obeying God remains. The Bible says we can expect no real success apart from it.

And there are still plenty of incentives for obeying God. Saul saw three prophecies fulfilled to the letter, but we can count fulfilled prophecies into the hundreds.

ONGOING TESTS

This also remains unchanged: we are all tested at this point of whether we will believe God's word and obey it.

The Bible affirms that there is no hope for eternal life apart from the saving work of Jesus Christ. But we live in a society that says such teaching must be dismissed. It is far too dogmatic and narrow! The test placed before each of us is whether we will believe the word of God or the dogmas of our time.

The test does not end after we have received Christ. The Bible tells us to believe its teachings and follow its commands. But our culture shouts that we are fools to do so. Christians constantly feel the pressure. Will we live on the basis of the bare word of God or cave in?

Saul failed the test and brought misery upon himself and those around him. May God help us to succeed where he failed.

For further study ▶

FOR FURTHER STUDY

1. The amazing chain of events that led Saul to Samuel demonstrates the sovereignty of God. Consider Proverbs 16:9; 19:21; 21:1, 30; Isaiah 43:13; 46:10. What do these verses teach about the sovereignty of God?

2. Read 1 Kings 22:28–37. What seemingly random act was actually determined by the sovereign God?

TO THINK ABOUT AND DISCUSS

1. The Bible offers hundreds of instances of fulfilled prophecies. List as many as you can think of and consider what they mean to you. How can we use these fulfilments to encourage our faith and to tell our friends and family members about the gospel?

2. What incentives do you have for obeying the Lord? Have there been 'coincidences' in your life—perhaps in your conversion or in other situations—where you now see that the hand of God was at work? How does the Lord use such things to keep us following and trusting in him? How can we use these things to help us when we are struggling in our faith?

10 Farewell, people!

1 Samuel 12:1–25

Israel had her new king, and now it was time for Samuel to lay down his responsibilities as the judge of the nation. He would continue serving in his capacities as priest and prophet, but the day-to-day responsibility of leading the nation would now fall upon the shoulders of Saul.

Samuel was not about to take his leave without addressing the people he so sincerely loved. So we have his farewell in this chapter.

SAMUEL DECLARES HIS FAITHFULNESS

Samuel shines from the pages of Scripture as an example of faithful service to the Lord. Called by God while a mere child, he now steps aside at an advanced age. And he is able fearlessly to ask if he has been anything less than totally faithful in his many years of service (v. 3). No one could find anything with which to accuse him (v. 4).

SAMUEL DECLARES GOD'S FAITHFULNESS

These verses consist of a sustained emphasis on how very faithful God had been to the nation of Israel. He raised up Moses and Aaron to deliver them from bondage in Egypt

(vv. 6,8). He proved to be faithful to them even when they were faithless, giving them various deliverers when their enemies rose up against them (vv. 9–11). He continued to be faithful to them even though they had strongly displeased him with their demand for a king (v. 12).

The upshot of it all is that the Lord had plenty of reasons to abandon them, but he had never given them so much as a single reason to abandon him. But he had never abandoned them, and they had abandoned him time after time.

SAMUEL CALLS FOR THEIR FAITHFULNESS

The proper way for them to respond to God's faithfulness to them was by faithfulness to him. They had to refuse to do in the future the type of thing they had done in demanding a king.

Samuel refused to tiptoe around their sin. He knew the well-being of the people demanded that they face their sin and turn from it.

To drive its seriousness home to their hearts, Samuel called upon the Lord to send thunder and rain (v. 17). This would have been extraordinary enough had God simply done it in response to Samuel's prayer, but it was even more striking because thunder and rain did not occur at that time of the year.

How did the people respond? Samuel had framed the matter in such a way that they had no room to manoeuvre. Thunder and rain would prove their sin, and the thunder and rain came! The people could only cry: 'Pray for your servants to the LORD your God, that we may not die; for we have added to all our sins the evil of asking a king for ourselves' (v. 19).

Samuel's response to this is quite astonishing. He did not try to lessen or diminish the gravity of their sins. He agreed with them that they had indeed acted very wickedly, but he added: 'Do not turn aside from following the LORD, but serve the LORD with all your heart' (v. 20).

So God's demand for service was not cancelled by their sin. The demand was still in place. It was ongoing. Their sin did not exempt them from service.

FAILURE NEED NOT BE FINAL

Samuel called the people of Israel to serve the Lord even though they had failed in obedience. What consolation there is here! Satan has a very long memory, and he makes it his business to cause the saints of God to have long memories as well—at least on this matter of sin. He is ever eager to assure us that our failures are final in kingdom work. Sin against God, and he has no more use for you! He puts you for ever on the shelf! You are done!

It is easy to understand the strategy. Satan has a vested interest in putting every child of God on the sidelines of service.

And he also enjoys slandering God, and, make no mistake, the suggestion that failure is final is a slander. It suggests that our sin is greater than all God's grace. But just the opposite is true! God's grace is greater than our sin!

We could ask Simon Peter about it. No one failed more miserably than he. Three times—count them!—he denied the Lord Jesus. Not once, not twice, but three times! Once would have been incredibly foul and vile, but three!

In his darkest moments, when the spectre of those denials rose to haunt him, Simon must have concluded that the Lord was through with him. It was not so! There is the Lord Jesus in John 21 pursuing his disciple! And there he is restoring him to usefulness! And there in Acts 2 is that same disciple standing boldly to declare the glorious gospel of Christ! And there are 3000 souls being saved!

God's people are guilty of great wickedness when they refuse to obey the Lord, but they only make the wickedness greater when they use it as an excuse to sit instead of serve.

THE MEANING OF SERVICE

Begin talking about serving the Lord and it won't be long before someone sidles up to say: 'To my way of thinking, I am serving the Lord.'

Behind such words is the assumption that we determine what constitutes service to God. But we don't set the standard of service and then seek to live up to our own standard. God sets it, and we are called to measure up to it.

How does God define service? We can isolate three components from Samuel's words. Let's think of it in terms of a river that flows from a spring through a channel and empties into the ocean. Service to God has a spring, a channel and an ocean.

Its spring is the fear of God (vv. 14,24). What does this mean? It is regarding God with such awe and wonder that we desire to obey him, and dread displeasing him by refusing to obey.

While service springs from the fear of God, it flows through the channel of the heart. Twice Samuel exhorts his listeners to service with their whole hearts (vv. 20,24).

Our service is, then, to correspond to the teaching of the apostle Paul, who says we are to be 'not lagging in diligence, fervent in spirit, serving the Lord' (Romans 12:11). The apostle was able to say that he himself served with his 'spirit' in the gospel of Christ (Romans 1:9). Service to God that doesn't come from the heart is not really service to God at all.

The ocean into which service empties is obedience to God. In verse 14, Samuel links serving the Lord with obeying the voice of the Lord. There can be no service where there is not obedience.

And where do we hear the voice of the Lord? Many claim to hear it whispering within, but we must be very careful here! How often we hear what we want to hear and attribute it to God! Samuel forged a link between the Lord's voice and what the Lord had caused to be written—his commandments! Obedience is not paying heed to vague and slippery hunches. It is ordering our lives according to the written word of God.

THE BLESSING OF SERVICE

God demands our service, not because he needs anything from us (Job 35:5–7), but rather because we need it. We need to serve God to find true fulfilment in life. We are so constituted that we must serve a god. If we do not serve the true God, we will serve false gods.

And what happens when we serve such gods? Samuel leaves no doubt about the answer. Those who go after false gods will find nothing in them because there is nothing to find. Those gods are empty nothings, and they have no power to help us (v. 21).

In serving the true God, we stay away from all the pretenders who have nothing to offer, and we find what Samuel calls 'the good and the right way' (v. 23).

Most of us would admit that serving the Lord is the right thing, but we have never yet fully come to appreciate that it is also the good thing. But Samuel lashes these two things inseparably together and drives us to the conclusion that what is right is also what is good.

THE PRIVILEGE OF SERVICE

Service to God! Our hearts should leap at the very thought. God allows us to serve him!

Why should we be thrilled about this? Samuel called the attention of his hearers to two things. First, he pointed to the marvel of God making them his people (v. 22). He then called their attention to the tremendous things God had done for them (v. 24).

In making them his people, God had first blessed them with the greatest single blessing he had to bestow. And, mark it well, the reason he had done so was because it 'pleased' him (v. 22). There was nothing in them to commend them in any way to God. He had not made them his because they were a cut above other people. They were made of the same sinful, sorry stuff as everybody else. It was rather a matter of the sovereign God dipping into that stuff to bring out a people, and, in so doing, bringing glory to his grace and power and wisdom.

Nothing has changed in the way in which people become God's people. It is all due to his grace. Every child of God is a debtor to that which chose him in eternity past, made him know his sinful condition and enabled him to believe in the Saviour, the Lord Jesus Christ. And that same powerful grace will, as Samuel pointed out, not allow the Lord to 'forsake his people' (v. 22). It is grace that reaches from eternity to eternity, that is, eternity past to eternity future. It was all planned in the former, and it will all issue into the latter.

This same grace is sufficient for the children of God as they make their way to the glory that awaits them. God does not withhold from them one thing that they need but blesses them with every spiritual blessing so that at each and every point of their lives believers can 'consider' the 'great things' the Lord has done for them (v. 24).

God, then, not only blesses his people with the greatest of all blessings—salvation through Christ—but provides blessing on top of blessing.

Sadly enough, God's people have trouble with serving him just as Samuel's people did. What is wrong with us? Nothing that a long look at the glorious privilege of being visited by the grace of God would not cure. May God help us to bask in the glory of it all until his service becomes our delight and passion!

FOR FURTHER STUDY

1. Joshua 24:1–25 serves as another example of a farewell address. What did Joshua emphasize in this message?
2. Read Acts 20:17–38 for a similar style of speech. What were the main points made by Paul?

TO THINK ABOUT AND DISCUSS

1. How does Samuel's emphasis on his own faithfulness challenge your own walk with the Lord?
2. In what ways does Samuel's emphasis on God's faithfulness help and encourage us, e.g. in hard personal financial circumstances, in difficult family situations, in a struggling church?

11 Saul giving Samuel grief

1 Samuel 13:1–15

Samuel wrapped up his farewell address to Israel with words that were absolutely plain: 'Only fear the LORD, and serve him in truth with all your heart; for consider what great things he has done for you. But if you still do wickedly, you shall be swept away, both you and your king' (12:24–25).

The people had demanded a king for themselves so they could be like the nations around them, but these words show that God was still king in Israel. The success of the people and their king depended on them recognizing this and obeying the Lord.

In other words, the people of Israel were still to be governed by the word of God. It was the job of the new king to make sure the nation's affairs were conducted accordingly. If the word of God was heard and obeyed, all would go well with the people and their king. On the other hand, if they were to take God's word lightly, they would come to calamity. It was as simple as that.

SAUL IS TESTED

In these verses we find Saul being tested at this very point.

Would he heed the word of God and adhere to it regardless of the cost? Or would he place his own wisdom above that word?

The test came to Saul in this form: before going into battle against the Philistines, he was to wait at Gilgal for seven days until Samuel came to offer a sacrifice to the Lord and to show him, Saul, what he was to do.

No one could have been better prepared for a test. First, Saul knew from the time he was anointed that this test was going to come in this form (10:8). To be forewarned is to be forearmed! That is how it is supposed to work! Saul was forewarned. But how did he know that Samuel was telling the truth about this test? How did he know that Samuel was truly declaring the word of God?

Samuel also dealt with this problem. The very same day he warned Saul about this test, he gave him three detailed prophecies, and he declared that they would all come true that very day. Each did (10:1–13)!

All of that should have been more than enough to convince Saul that the word of God as spoken by Samuel could be trusted completely. But Saul received even more confirmation. Some of it came when he was publicly chosen by the casting of lots. That random act resulted in his selection, just as Samuel had indicated privately.

And then Saul stood with the people when it thundered and rained during the wheat harvest (12:17). This was unprecedented. It never thundered or rained at that time. But when Samuel called upon the Lord to confirm his words, it both thundered and rained!

All of this should have made an indelible impression on Saul. He should have said to himself: 'This man Samuel speaks the word of God which is powerful and true, and when my day of testing comes, the day of which Samuel has spoken, I am going to do as he has commanded. I am going to wait, no matter what!'

The day of testing finally arrived. The well-being of the nation and Saul's own well-being hinged on him yielding to the word of God and showing that he understood that the nation must be governed by it.

SAUL FAILS

Saul almost made it. Six days came and went, and he refused to jump the gun. The seventh day dawned. This was the day Samuel had promised to come. Saul probably expected Samuel to arrive early that morning. The nation was, after all, facing a severe crisis. But morning passed and Samuel had not appeared. Surely, he would come early in the afternoon, but no!

Saul now found himself under enormous pressure. A clear word on one hand and a great crisis on the other! What to do? Finally, Saul felt he could wait no longer. It was true that the day was not over, but it looked as if Samuel had failed. Something had to be done! So Saul commanded that the sacrifice be brought, and he offered it. Just as he finished offering the sacrifice, Samuel came strolling down the pathway. The old man had not failed after all.

One glance at the prophet told Saul that he had made a grave error. Immediately he started fumbling for an explanation. Six simple words perfectly capture the reason he thought he could disregard the word of God: 'When I saw ... then I said' (vv. 11–12).

What had Saul seen? Philistines! He could not even close his eyes without seeing a horde of swarming Philistines. Why? Verses 2 and 3 provide the answer. Saul had mustered a small army, a portion of which, under his son Jonathan, had defeated a Philistine garrison at Geba. That had thoroughly enraged the Philistines, and they began gathering their forces for a massive attack on Israel.

Then there was something else Saul saw. Not in his mind's eye, but in reality! Wherever he looked, he saw fear and panic among his own people. The Philistines had not yet launched their attack, but some had already found hiding places (v. 6). Others had fled across the Jordan River (v. 7). And those who remained were quaking in their sandals (v. 7).

Powerful, ferocious Philistines and feeble, scared Israelites! What a combination! And what a dilemma for Saul! And Saul, forgetting that God can do the impossible (12:17), reasoned that his only hope lay in mounting a surprise attack on the Philistines while they were still gathering their army. But how could he launch such an attack if he had to wait, wait, wait?

So his seeing led to his saying. And what did he say? Essentially this: SOMETHING MUST BE DONE NOW! In other words, the seeing of difficult circumstances led Saul to rely on his own wisdom instead of on the word of God. His seeing led him to doubt and distrust. There is nothing wrong with human wisdom per se, but there is something wrong with it when it conflicts with God's word.

REJOICE IN THE RELIABILITY OF GOD'S WORD

As Saul had ample evidence for believing that Samuel was declaring the word of God, so we have plenty of evidence for believing the Bible is the word of God. Several things could be mentioned—the fulfilment of prophecies, archaeological discoveries, the unity of the Bible, the changed lives of those who have received the Bible's message, the Bible's capacity for weathering attacks.

The foremost evidence for the utter reliability of the Bible is the testimony of Jesus, who put his stamp of approval upon the whole of Scripture. This means a couple of things. The Old Testament was completed years before Jesus began his earthly ministry, but the writing of the New Testament did not even begin until after his death on the cross. To put his stamp of approval on all of Scripture means, then, that he had to endorse the Old Testament as it existed and to pre-endorse the New Testament.

He did the former by appealing to it to settle debates (Matthew 4:1–11; 22:23–33), by explicitly affirming its trustworthiness (Matthew 5:17–18; John 10:35) and by endorsing those persons and events that are often doubted (Matthew 12:39–41; 19:4–5; 24:37–39; Luke 4:25–27; 17:28–32).

Jesus pre-endorsed the writing of the New Testament by assuring his disciples that the Holy Spirit would provide each of these needed elements. He would call things to their remembrance (John 14:26), he would guide them into truth (John 16:13) and he would even disclose things to come (John 16:13).

So no matter where you turn in Scripture you may rest assured that Jesus Christ has initialled every page!

AVOID THE 'SAUL SYNDROME'

We live in a day of mustering Philistines and fleeing Israelites.

Never, it seems, have the devil's wolves been more wolfish and the Lord's sheep more sheepish. Our temptation, like Saul's, is to let the difficulty of our circumstances cause us to rely on our own wisdom.

The Bible says the gospel of Christ is 'the power of God to salvation for everyone who believes' (Romans 1:16). Modern Philistines ridicule this. They confidently assure us that humanity is not God's special creation but made up of highly developed animals that came about through a cosmic accident. They further affirm that while human beings are animals, they are very good animals. They are not standing under the condemnation of a holy God and do not need his salvation.

Give these highly developed animals a good education, a sound environment and government programmes, and their goodness will shine brilliantly. And the only thing from which they need salvation is this teaching that people are sinful and need God!

If, for the sake of the argument, people do need salvation from sin, it is sheer lunacy, they allege, to believe such a thing could be provided by a man dying on a Roman cross outside Jerusalem over 2000 years ago.

We cannot expect Philistines to be anything other than Philistines. We cannot expect those who do not know God to act as if they did, or to cheer us on while we proclaim his message. Philistines have always been Philistines and always will be.

Neither should we tremble, flee and hide every time a Philistine rattles his sabre! We must not jettison the doctrines of Scripture merely because the modern Philistines reject them. We must not stop preaching the message that we were created in the image of God, that sin has defaced and marred that image, that we cannot be educated out of sin but can be forgiven it and restored to God through the death of Jesus on the cross.

The truth is that many Israelites are trembling these days. We fear we will be laughing stocks in a sophisticated age. So we load our sermons with good humour and clever witticisms. And we talk very little about sin, judgement and repentance, and much about self-esteem and managing the problems life brings our way.

Saul was caught between militant Philistines and weak Israelites, and he caved in. Having the opportunity to stand squarely for God's truth, he failed.

Because he refused to take his stand on the word of God, he could not rightly govern people who were called to live on the basis of that word. So his reign was doomed to ineffectiveness, and his throne would not be passed on to his children.

Each and every child of God trembles either before this intimidating world or before God's word (Isaiah 66:2). And each of us, like Saul, must decide which we will do. Saul made the wrong decision. With God's help, we must make the right one.

FOR FURTHER STUDY

1. Study 2 Peter 1:19–21. Where do we find the word of God today? How does the apostle Peter describe God's word?
2. Consider 2 Timothy 3:14–17. What does the apostle Paul teach about Scripture?

TO THINK ABOUT AND DISCUSS

1. Why is it important for you to obey the Bible? What should be our attitude to the Bible? Think about the dangers of toning the message down when we speak to people who are not Christians. What must we do to avoid this?
2. What are some of the things that pressure you to disobey God's word? Are there particular things that get in the way of you reading it and obeying it? Consider points such as: pressure at work; television; use of media such as computers. How might you develop a personal strategy (or with your family) to overcome these kinds of pressures?

12 Saul giving Samuel grief again

1 Samuel 15:1–35

We have all botched assignments at one time or another because we were not clear on what we were supposed to do. King Saul of Israel had a different problem. The clearer the assignment, the more he botched it. The episode at Gilgal was one example. The above passage presents another.

SAUL'S DUTY

These verses tell us that Saul again had absolute clarity. God sent Samuel to him to command him to utterly obliterate the Amalekites.

Many who profess to be deeply disturbed that God would command such a thing feel no squeamishness at all about the liquidation of millions of the unborn! But let's deal with this question: Why would God command the execution of the Amalekites? The answer is that he is a holy God who is extremely zealous for his glory and the good of his people.

The Amalekites, on the other hand, were a tremendously bloodthirsty, cruel people who had absolutely no qualms about butchering the women and children of other nations. When the nation of Israel was making her way out of bondage in Egypt, the Amalekites lay in wait for them and attacked the rear of their procession where the feeble, the faint and the weary were concentrated (Exodus 17:8–16; Deuteronomy 25:17–19).

Why did they do this? The Amalekites were themselves descendants of Abraham (Amalek was the grandson of Esau). As such, they knew about the special calling that God had placed upon Israel, and they hated and despised it. In that hatred of Israel, the people of Amalek were transparently saying that they hated the grace of God at work in Israel.

But let's get back to our story. Saul had a distinct command from God. Like it or not, it was clear.

SAUL'S FAILURE

But Saul's problem with clear assignments kicked in again. His entire life can be summarized like this: clear commands and constant compromise.

This time Saul's compromise consisted of sparing the king of Amalek and some of the cattle and sheep.

SAUL'S EXCUSES

No matter how glaring his failure, Saul was never lacking a way to avoid facing it. First, he denied it. As soon as he saw Samuel, he said: 'Blessed are you of the LORD! I have performed the commandment of the Lord' (v. 13). But Samuel was no fool. The lowing of the cattle and the bleating of the sheep told him otherwise (v. 14). So Saul changed his tune by blaming the people (vv. 15,21). He then moved to his final excuse. Yes, he had disobeyed, but it was for a good reason, namely, sacrificing to the Lord (v. 21).

I didn't do it. I couldn't help it. I had a good reason. Sound familiar? We all have the tendency to take refuge in such flimsy excuses when confronted with our sin.

I've been saying Saul had a problem with clear assignments. The unvarnished truth is he had an obedience problem, and that is another way of saying he had a heart problem. He had trouble with obedience to God because his heart was not right with God. There was no room in Saul's heart for God because it was already filled with himself. The monument he built for himself after attacking the Amalekites tells us all we need to know about his heart (v. 12).

SAMUEL'S RESPONSE

Samuel was not impressed with Saul's manoeuvring. He first pointed Saul to an undying principle—nothing is more important to God than obedience. There can be no substitute for it. If we are not willing to give God obedience, it does not matter how many other things we are willing to give him (v. 22).

Samuel then proceeded to point Saul to the essence of disobedience. It is of one piece with witchcraft and idolatry (v. 23).

Finally, Samuel pointed Saul to the costliness of disobedience. What a big price Saul paid for his rebellion! His prior disobedience at Gilgal had resulted in God declaring that his kingdom would not continue. None of his sons would ever sit on his throne (13:14). Now another dimension is added. Saul was himself rejected by the Lord as king (v. 26). This did not mean he would be immediately removed. As a matter of fact, he continued to reign for several years. But he was rejected while he reigned! He held the office without the blessing of God!

The frightening fulfilment of Samuel's words is found in

these words: 'But the Spirit of the LORD departed from Saul, and a distressing spirit from the LORD troubled him' (16:14).

What a tragic figure this Saul is! His story is here so that we will learn the lesson of obedience and thus avoid sharing his tragedy.

THE DANGER OF CREATING OUR OWN GOD

Many profess to be very disturbed by God calling for the obliteration of the Amalekites. Such a thing is out of keeping with their notion of God. But we must accept God as he reveals himself in Scripture or we will fall into the trap of creating our own God. And God reveals himself in Scripture as the God of judgement!

We must also understand that the episodes of judgement in Scripture have a merciful intent behind them. God has severely judged a few in the long march of history that all might be warned of the final judgement day when his holiness will be made terribly apparent. The Amalekites join Noah's generation, Sodom and Gomorrah, and Ananias and Sapphira as powerful warnings of the eternal judgement that awaits all who rebel against God.

When some pointed out to the Lord Jesus that Pilate had butchered some Galileans, Jesus responded: 'I tell you, … unless you repent you will all likewise perish' (Luke 13:5). He was not suggesting that Pilate would liquidate all who failed to repent. Rather he was saying that this tragedy was a harbinger of the far greater tragedy that lies ahead of those who refuse to repent.

John Piper catches Jesus' meaning in these words: 'Man-centred humans are amazed that God should withhold life and joy from his creatures. But the God-centred Bible is amazed that God should withhold judgement from sinners.'[1]

THE DANGER OF WRITING OUR OWN BIBLE

Samuel equated Saul's disobedience with witchcraft and idolatry. How did he get from disobedience to such things? Think about it. The goal of witchcraft is to gain truth apart from God's revelation. When we rebel against God we are essentially thumbing our noses at his commands and seeking to write our own Scripture.

THE DANGER OF DEIFYING OURSELVES

On what basis did Samuel liken Saul's sins to idolatry? Idolatry is putting something else in the place of God and giving to it the allegiance that belongs to God. When we stubbornly refuse to listen to God and insist on going our own way, we are declaring ourselves and our desires to be our god and are worshipping them.

For further study ▶

FOR FURTHER STUDY

1. God's command to Saul to eliminate the Amalekites is emblematic of his command regarding other nations. Why did God want these nations destroyed? Read Leviticus 18:24–30 and Deuteronomy 12:31; 18:9–14.

2. Read Revelation 20:11–15. What do these verses tell us about the final judgement?

TO THINK ABOUT AND DISCUSS

1. What is your response to the truth that God is a just judge? Does it make you fear him? How does it encourage you to trust him? Is it possible and right to both fear and trust God?

2. What are some excuses people are using today for disobeying God? Have you made excuses in the past? Are there areas in your life where you are still making excuses: in use of money, use of TV, use of time, etc?

Notes

1. **John Piper,** *The Supremacy of God in Preaching* (Grand Rapids: Baker Book House, 1990), p. 30.

13 A future king

1 Samuel 16:1–13

The Lord shows mercy to his people. Not a single day goes by that is not edged with his blessings. But there are times when the Lord decides to smile more graciously upon his people. Such a time came in Israel of old when God gave her David. God never smiled more broadly in Old Testament times than he did at that time.

What an incredible man David was! What a blessing for Israel! A warrior to fight her battles, a king to lead her to unprecedented glory, an inspired poet to fill her worship with songs of praise: David was all this and more.

GOD SPEAKS TO SAMUEL

As this chapter opens, we find the nation of Israel in a wretched condition. Her king, Saul, had massively demonstrated his unfitness to rule. Though called to be the leader of the people of God, he had made it clear he had no heart for God. Saul's aversion to the things of God cast a spiritual chill over the land. The prophet Samuel deeply mourned Saul's lack of spiritual vitality, and the Lord 'regretted' making Saul king (15:35).

The people themselves were far from the Lord. Their desire

to be like other nations (8:5,20) indicated a shocking elevation of worldly standards over God's revealed will (8:10–20).

It was against this backdrop that God spoke to Samuel these words: 'Fill your horn with oil, and go; I am sending you to Jesse the Bethlehemite. For I have provided myself a king among his sons' (v. 1).

'I have provided myself a king.' The king of Israel was to be for God himself. He was to rule on God's behalf and in accordance with his will. Saul had miserably failed to be God's king, but God, speaking of the future as already accomplished (such is his sovereign power), said he had provided a king who would not fail.

SAMUEL FINDS DAVID

Samuel arrived at Jesse's house and invited his sons to attend the sacrifice (v. 5). When Samuel saw Jesse's firstborn, Eliab, he was duly impressed. Eliab was tall and striking in every way.

But God said: 'Do not look at his appearance or at his physical stature, because I have refused him. For the LORD does not see as man sees; for man looks at the outward appearance, but the Lord looks at the heart' (v. 7). Thus rebuked, Samuel doesn't seem to have jumped to any more conclusions as the sons of Jesse passed by. The second, the third, the fourth ... all the way through to the seventh! All were paraded before Samuel, and still there was no king.

Samuel was puzzled. The word of the Lord was clear. There was a king among Jesse's sons, but he was not to be found among these seven men. There had to be another. So Samuel asked Jesse: 'Are all the young men here?' And Jesse's response seems to amount to saying: 'Well, there's the youngest who is out keeping the sheep, but, surely you wouldn't be interested in him?' (v. 11).

But God was interested in him, and, when David arrived on the scene, the Lord said to Samuel: 'Arise, anoint him; for this is the one!' (v. 12).

We shouldn't picture God in these verses as a frustrated shopper who goes over item after item and finally has to settle on something because nothing else strikes his fancy. David was the one whom God sent Samuel to anoint. Why David? Because, even though he was not as striking physically as Eliab, he had the right heart. Why was his heart right for what lay ahead? Because God, in grace, had already put the right things in his heart!

We are surprised that Samuel needed to be cautioned about looking on the outward appearance. If anyone shouldn't have been taken in with outward appearance it was Samuel. Saul was an imposing and striking physical specimen (10:23), but he had turned out to be a spiritual pygmy, and Samuel had seen all of this from a front-row seat.

LIVING EXPECTANTLY

The life of David will cause us to say: 'If God so smiled upon his people then, perhaps he will be pleased to smile more broadly upon us.'

One thing ought to be clear as day to us. We urgently need that broader smile. Our nations continue their steady march into ruin. Our churches are wracked with dissension, turmoil, and apathy. Homes, even Christian homes, continue to disintegrate. Christians easily succumb to the prevailing moods and mores of the day.

What's the problem? We may rightly trace much of our trouble to an inept, ineffective church. But why is the church so inept and ineffective? Some suggest it's because she doesn't have the right programmes or methods, that the church machinery is not functioning as it should and a little tinkering with it will produce the desired results.

The real problem, however, can be put as baldly as this—the church is ineffective because God has hidden his face from her. She has grieved him and he is withholding his power and blessing.

It appears that many are beginning to see that the great need of the church is revival. Revival is the work of God, not the work of man. We cannot produce it just by pressing a few buttons. We are completely shut up until God's own time if we are to have the revival we so urgently need. Revival is God taking the initiative. It is God breaking into the lives of his apathetic and indifferent people to bring new vigour and strength.

One aspect of revival is reformation. Thomas J. Nettles defines this as 'the recovery of biblical truth which leads to the purifying of one's theology. It involves a rediscovery of the Bible as the judge and guide of all thought and action, corrects errors in interpretation, gives precision, coherence, and courage to doctrinal confession, and gives form and energy to the corporate worship of the Triune God.'[1]

The fact that revival is God' s work doesn't mean we should just sit on our hands and do nothing. There are a couple of glistening truths in this sixteenth chapter of 1 Samuel on this matter of when God's people can realistically expect him to smile more broadly upon them. If we are willing to occupy the ground described here, we will have much more reason to hope revival is near than we will if we refuse to occupy it.

LIVING WITH AWARENESS

From these verses, we can say that when God intends great mercy for his people he first fills them with a sense of burden and heaviness over the conditions in which they find themselves. In other words, God gives his people an awareness of the evil of the times.

This always seems to be God's 'modus operandi'. History is replete with instances in which it looked as if all was hopeless and then God moved in to unleash a fresh burst of mercy upon his people.

We want to know if we are near such a burst today, but that's the wrong question for us to be asking. The right question is this—do we feel the evil of the times? Are we burdened and distressed over the condition of the church today? Until we get burdened we need not scan the horizon for the thunderclouds of God's mercy. They only break upon the heads of those who feel the burden of the times. We have no right to expect the mercy drops of revival if we are content lightly to dismiss the evil of our time by saying: 'Our time is no worse than other times. We just hear more about the evil.' We have no right to expect the showers of blessing if we are content to believe our problems are political in nature and can be straightened out at the next election.

Samuel mourned over Saul and what he had unleashed upon Israel, and we may be sure other godly Israelites mourned as well. How many mourn today? But did not God tell Samuel not to mourn over Saul (v. 1)? Yes, but it was only when he was ready to give David to the nation. We also can stop our mourning, then, when revival breaks loose.

LIVING WITH THE GOD OF SURPRISES

When God intends great mercy for his people, he invariably bypasses those things on which we are most likely to depend (vv. 6–13).

The fact that Samuel needed to be cautioned about looking on outward appearances tells us how inclined we are to rely upon mere human wisdom when it comes to the things of God. Start talking about the crying need of the hour for revival and someone will invariably pop up to suggest a committee be appointed to study the need and bring back a recommendation. Someone else will suggest we bring in a Christian rock group, a movie star, or an athlete with 'a good testimony'. Someone else will chime in with a suggestion that we do a study of the demographics of the community and plan a multimedia campaign that will arrest attention.

It should be obvious to all of us by now that these things have been tried and have failed. We have seen what human wisdom can produce, and it's not much. But, like Samuel, we still have the tendency to flirt with Eliab even though we have been burned by Saul.

How differently God does things! Throughout the running centuries, he has consistently sent revival to his people through unlikely, ordinary instruments.

God did the same thing when he sent his Son into this world. Jesus came, not to the hustle and bustle of Jerusalem, but to tiny Bethlehem. And when Jesus began his public ministry, he bypassed those who were the movers and shakers of the day and surrounded himself with ordinary fishermen and tax-collectors.

God's saving work to this very day is primarily carried on in those who are not mighty or noble but who are weak and plain. Why? Paul gives the answer. It's so all the glory for his mighty works will go to him rather than to men (1 Corinthians 1:29).

We can be sure God will protect his glory as much in his reviving work as he does in his saving work. He will not allow us to take a shred of it for ourselves, and we would do exactly that if we could produce a revival through our stars, our promotions, and our committees.

But with all our slickness and cleverness, we have been unable to produce what we so desperately need, namely, a true work of God in our midst. Maybe, just maybe, God has almost brought us to the end of ourselves so we can now stand in awe of the mercy he is about to unleash upon us.

For further study ▶

FOR FURTHER STUDY

1. Look at 1 Corinthians 1:26–31. How does Paul apply God's delight in doing the unexpected? What is Paul's conclusion about this?
2. Find 1 Samuel 13:14 and Acts 13:22,36. How do these verses characterize King David?

TO THINK ABOUT AND DISCUSS

1. What does it mean to you that God often uses unlikely people to do his work? Can you think of people in the past who have been used by God, yet who seemed unlikely? What do we mean by 'unlikely'? Who are the people who are really, in God's eyes, unlikely to do his work?
2. What can you do to seek true revival? How should we respond to the need for revival in these days? Is it enough just to pray?

Notes

1. **Thomas J. Nettles,** 'A Better Way: Reformation and Revival' in *Reformation & Revival*, ed. John H. Armstrong (1992), vol. i, no. 2, pp. 23–24.

14 A surprising appearance

1 Samuel 28:1–25

The first verse of 1 Samuel 25 reports the death of Samuel in the briefest and starkest terms: 'Then Samuel died.' That fact is repeated again in the chapter before us: 'Now Samuel had died' (v. 3). That would seem to be the end of Samuel's time on this earth, but it wasn't to be. No, Samuel's body was not raised from its grave, but he did make another appearance on the stage of human history.

The gripping account of this is found in 1 Samuel 28. King Saul was in dire straits. The Philistines were mustering their forces to launch an all-out attack on Israel, and Saul's heart 'trembled greatly' (1 Samuel 28:5).

THE SILENCE

Saul sought guidance from the Lord whom he had so long ago driven away, but the Lord refused to answer. Saul, more desperate than he had ever been, disguised himself and went to a witch in En Dor. The disguise was necessary. Saul had driven the spiritists and mediums from the land (28:3), and the woman would not even have been willing to admit she was a witch if she saw Saul standing on her doorstep.

Once in the witch's house, Saul asked her to bring Samuel's

spirit back. The irony is heavy. Saul now wants to hear from the very Samuel to whom he had so often refused to listen!

THE SÉANCE

The woman, still unaware of the identity of her visitor, agreed to bring Samuel up, but she was shocked when Samuel actually appeared. It is obvious that she was not expecting him.

We can understand her shock only if we realize the sleight of hand that took place in her normal séance. The witch, who was in contact with and under the control of an evil spirit, would go into a trance. The evil spirit would then take control of her and impersonate the one who was supposedly being called up.

But this séance would be far different from any the woman had previously conducted. God stepped in and took over. He actually caused the spirit of Samuel to appear, and simultaneously made the woman realize her visitor was Saul. This was a séance gone awry. No wonder she was shocked!

THE SENTENCE

The witch is now replaced on centre stage by Samuel who directly addresses Saul: 'Why have you disturbed me by bringing me up?' (v. 15). Saul responds by pouring out his anguish. He desperately needed guidance for the facing of the Philistines, and God refused to help him in any way. He needed Samuel to tell him what to do (v.15).

Samuel had no words of comfort for this man who had made the Lord his enemy (v. 16). But he did have a word of reminder and a declaration of judgement. The reminder consisted of Samuel affirming that God was in the process of doing what he had promised to do, namely, give Saul's kingdom to David because of Saul's flagrant disobedience (vv. 17–18). The declaration of judgement consisted of Samuel announcing that Saul and his sons would be killed the very next day, and that the army of Israel would be defeated by the Philistines (v. 19).

In the space of mere moments, Saul went from complete silence to a devastating sentence. And both the silence and the sentence were his own doing. The author closes this sorrowful account with these words: 'Then they rose and went away that night' (v. 25). That night, dark as it was, could not equal the darkness of Saul's soul, and that darkness would lead him to the darkness of death.

All of this must surely make us think of another dark soul and another night. The dark soul? Judas Iscariot! The night? That night when Judas left Jesus and the other disciples for the purpose of carrying out his foul scheme of betrayal. John reports Judas' departure, and pregnantly adds: 'And it was night' (John 13:30).

And so it was!

LOOK TO THE END

Samuel was an extraordinary man of God. He will for ever be one of the heroes of the Christian faith. But as eminent as he was, he was not exempt from death.

We do well to think often about the end of our earthly journey. We each have an appointment with death (Hebrews 9:27). The reality and enormity of that appointment plainly tells us what is truly important. We must prepare to meet God, and we can do this only through receiving the Lord Jesus Christ as our Lord and Saviour.

If we have received Christ, we must faithfully serve him while we have time and opportunity, saying with the Lord himself: 'I must work the works of him who sent me while it is day; the night is coming when no one can work' (John 9:4).

LOOK AWAY FROM WITCHCRAFT

The fact that Saul went to a witch for guidance does not mean that the Bible endorses witchcraft. The author of 1 Samuel merely reports Saul's going as a fact. This does not encourage us to follow his example.

The teaching of Scripture is that witchcraft is one of 'the works of the flesh', and those who practise such works 'will not inherit the kingdom of God' (Galatians 5:19–21).

LOOK TO THE LIGHT

The day after Judas' betrayal the darkest darkness of all fell upon Jesus as he died on the cross. That darkness was both visible and invisible. The people around the cross could readily tell that they were standing in deep and impenetrable gloom, but they could not see the even deeper darkness that Jesus experienced within. That was the darkness of the wrath of God. Jesus bore it so that all who believe in him will never have to bear it. He bore the darkness of wrath to bring to his people the light of life.

For further study ▶

FOR FURTHER STUDY

1. What do Deuteronomy 18:9–14 and Galatians 5:20 teach about witchcraft?

2. Read 2 Peter 2:4,17; Jude 6,13. What has the Lord reserved for the demons and those who follow them?

TO THINK ABOUT AND DISCUSS

1. What does Samuel's surprising appearance tell us about God?

2. What do you understand Christ to have suffered on the cross (see Romans 3:21–26; 1 Peter 2:24)? How should the knowledge of his suffering impact on your life (see 1 Peter 2:21–23; Matthew 16:24)?

15 Face2face with Christ

As the Lord Jesus walked with two of his disciples towards Emmaus on the day of his resurrection, he began with 'Moses and all the Prophets' and 'expounded to them in all the Scriptures the things concerning himself' (Luke 24:27). Later that evening the risen Christ appeared to his eleven disciples in Jerusalem and said: 'All things must be fulfilled which were written in the Law of Moses and the Prophets and Psalms concerning me' (Luke 24:44).

The very fact that he arose from the grave means that he is the sovereign Lord. He knows what he is talking about! And he insists that the Old Testament is all about him. If, therefore, we consider the life of Samuel without any thought of Christ, we are breaking with the Lord Jesus himself.

But where are we to find Christ in the life of Samuel? I suggest that the latter gives us two very large and substantial pictures of the former.

SAMUEL PORTRAYS CHRIST THE PROPHET

In chapter 4, we found Samuel being called to the prophetic office. We are not left in doubt about this. It meant that Samuel was God's man to declare God's message (3:19–4:1).

All the prophets, including Samuel, foreshadowed the

coming of the true prophet—Jesus. The apostle Peter made this connection in no uncertain terms when he spoke to a crowd outside the temple in Jerusalem:

> For Moses truly said to the fathers, 'The LORD your God will raise up for you a Prophet like me from your brethren. Him you shall hear in all things, whatever he says to you. And it shall be that every soul who will not hear that Prophet shall be utterly destroyed from among the people. Yes, and all the prophets from Samuel and those who follow, as many as have spoken, have also foretold these days'
>
> (Acts 3:22–24).

Simon Peter was affirming that Jesus was the Prophet of whom the prophets spoke (Acts 3:26).

One of Jesus' primary tasks, then, was to fully and accurately declare the truth of God. He never failed to do this. He never compromised the truth or corrupted it. He never added to it or took away from it. He never bartered it away for popularity's sake.

On the other hand, he proclaimed the truth in such a powerful and riveting way that his hearers were very impressed and had to admit that he was a prophet (Matthew 7:28–29; 21:11; Luke 4:22; John 6:14; 7:40–52).

SAMUEL PORTRAYS CHRIST THE PRIEST

We now hit the rewind button and return to a verse to which we merely tipped our hats as we sped by. This verse consists of the Lord's promise to Eli to raise up 'a faithful priest' (2:35).

Of whom was the Lord speaking here? Who was this faithful priest? Many commentators are convinced that Zadok is the fulfilment. He came to the priesthood after Abiathar was deposed (1 Kings 2:27). Abiathar was, of course, the last of Eli's descendants to serve in the priesthood.

Zadok and his descendants can be regarded as the fulfilment of this promise because they faithfully discharged the duties of high priest from the time of Solomon to what we call the intertestamental period, that is, the time between the Old and New Testaments.

It should be apparent to us that Zadok had to be a faithful priest to fulfil this promise, and he was. But it should also be apparent to us that Zadok could not possibly exhaust the promise God made to Eli. After we say all the good things that we can possibly say about Zadok, there is still promise left! So we must look beyond Zadok for the ultimate fulfilment of this promise, and when we do, we can only see the Lord Jesus Christ.

He is the complete fulfilment of this promise on two grounds.

THE LORD JESUS IS THE TRULY FAITHFUL ONE

Zadok and his descendants were generally faithful, but not perfectly faithful. They failed in various ways because they were cut from the same sinful cloth as the rest of humanity.

But the Lord Jesus was perfect in faithfulness. The author of Hebrews writes: 'Consider the Apostle and High Priest of our confession, Christ Jesus, who was faithful to Him who appointed him' (Hebrews 3:1b–2a).

It was essential for Jesus to be sinless for a very obvious reason. He came to receive the penalty for sinners. If he had been guilty of sin himself, he would have had to receive the penalty for his sins and could not, therefore, have received the penalty in the place of others.

THE LORD JESUS IS THE TRULY EVERLASTING ONE

The promise given to Eli was that God would give to his faithful priest 'a sure house', that is, one that would not pass away. Further, God promised that this faithful priest would 'walk before [his] anointed for ever'. In other words, the Lord was affirming that this faithful priest would walk 'as his anointed for ever'.

Every human priest is mortal, and their priesthood temporary, but Christ is eternal and his priesthood everlasting (Hebrews 7:23–28).

Matthew Henry writes of God's promise to Eli: 'It has its full accomplishment in the priesthood of Christ, that merciful and faithful high priest whom God raised up when the Levitical priesthood was thrown off, who in all things did his father's mind, and for whom God will build a sure house, build it on a rock, so that the gates of hell cannot prevail against it.'[1]

We cannot be 'face2face' with Samuel, then, without simultaneously being 'face2face' with Christ, because Samuel, as both prophet and priest, anticipates the Lord Jesus.

HEARING CHRIST THE PROPHET

We should not think that the prophesying of Jesus has ceased. Scripture is nothing less than the Lord himself declaring to us his truth, and the responsibility resting on us with the Bible is the same as that which rested on those who heard Jesus during his ministry, that is, to hear carefully (Matthew 17:5). Through the apostle Peter, the Lord God tells us that we do well to pay heed to Scripture 'as a light that shines in a dark place' (2 Peter 1:19).

In the Bible, we have nothing less than our glorious Lord

declaring glorious truth. Let us be aware of our blessing (Revelation 1:3) and beware of taking it for granted (Hebrews 5:11).

DEPENDING ON CHRIST THE PRIEST

Ours is a time in which it is permissible to speak about God but not about Jesus. Because all religions supposedly worship the same God, we can speak about him without offending anyone. But the name of Jesus is different! The mere mention of his name suggests that there is only way to salvation. The name of God is generic, but the name of Jesus is a particular brand! Why must we insist on Jesus? The answer is that he alone is the high priest!

The Bible teaches that we cannot have a relationship with God unless our sins are removed. The only way for sin to be removed is for its penalty to be paid. And what is the penalty for sin? It is the eternal wrath of God.

On the cross, Jesus paid that penalty. There he filled the office of high priest. He offered himself as the sacrifice for sinners. He stood in their place and took their penalty. He was both the sacrificing priest and the sacrifice itself. He offered himself on behalf of sinners.

More specifically, the Lord Jesus offered himself as the 'propitiation' for sin. To 'propitiate' is to satisfy or appease. The wrath of God against our sins had to be appeased in order for us to be forgiven, and the one way for that wrath to be satisfied was for its penalty to be carried out. On the cross, the wrath of God flamed out in Jesus. Because Jesus received it, no wrath remains for those who believe in Jesus.

The urgent business before each of us is to make sure that we have taken home to our hearts the truth declared by Christ the prophet and received the sacrifice offered by Christ the priest. If we refuse to do these things, we shall find ourselves 'face2face' with Christ the judge.

FOR FURTHER STUDY

1. Read John 4:1–25. How did the woman of Samaria respond to the Lord Jesus?

2. Study Hebrews 2:17; 4:15; 5:1,4–5,10. What was necessary so that Jesus could be the high priest of his people?

TO THINK ABOUT AND DISCUSS

1. Why do you think it was important for the Lord Jesus to live without sin? How does it encourage us to know that he did that?

2. What is your response to the Lord Jesus as God's faithful prophet and priest (see Hebrews 7:2–28; 1 John 2:1)?

Notes

1. **Matthew Henry,** *Matthew Henry's Commentary,* (Fleming H. Revell Publishing Co., n.d.), vol. ii, p. 294.